THE BAKUNDU OF CAMEROON YESTERDAY AND TODAY

A Study in Tradition and Modernity

Joseph B. Ebune

The Bakundu of Cameroon Yesterday and Today
Joseph B. Ebune

First published by

Miraclaire Academic Publications
Kansas City, (MO) USA
Website: www.miraclairepublishing.com
Email: info@miraclairepublishing.com

ISBN-13: 978-0692298121
ISBN-10: 0692298126

All rights reserved.
No part of this publication may be reproduced by any means, graphic, electronic, or mechanical, including photocopying, recording, taping or by any information storage retrieval system without the prior written permission of the copyright holder, except in the case of brief quotations embodied in critical articles and reviews.

© 2014 Miraclaire Academic Publications

Printed in the United States of America

Miraclaire Publishing makes every effort to ensure the accuracy of all the information ("Content") in its publications. However, Miraclaire and its agents and licensors make no representations or warranties whatsoever as to the accuracy, completeness, or suitability for any purpose of the Content and disclaim all such representations and warranties, whether expressed or implied to the maximum extent permitted by law. Any views expressed in this publication are the views of the author and are not necessarily the views of Miraclaire.

PREFACE

This study is essentially about culture and culture change in Bakundu society. Culture and culture change have assumed a new importance in recent years with the coming of globalisation, giving currency to phrases like "culture wars" and most famously, Huntington's "clash of civilisations", the latter symbolised by the current confrontations between radical Islam and a post-Christian, post-modern secular West.

This work examines the various dimensions of change in Bakundu belief system and practices. It shows how the process of modernization became irreversible because it was eventually embraced and sustained by new social classes which emerged through elite formations like the Bakundu Students' Union.

Among the Bakundu culture contact and culture change entered a new phase when Europeans – Missionaries, traders, colonial administrators and adventurers made contact with them, indirectly during the era of the slave trade and directly under colonial rule. The more direct contact came with the introduction of legitimate trade in the nineteenth century that officially ended the slave trade. The Bakundu now sold tropical commodities like palm oil to Europeans. But greater contact with Europeans was during colonial era when the Bakundu and other Africans became subject to Europeans and lost their political and social and cultural autonomy.

The work is an outgrowth of my doctoral dissertation. I was motivated to transform it into a book, having seen Bakundu cultural experience in modern times which has many sides resulting from encounters with European cultures which have modified Bakundu cultural values, beliefs and institutions. As a native speaker of the Bakundu language, I felt challenged to try to answer my own questions about it and how it works during my post-graduate studies by looking at the history of African-European contact before and under colonialism, and the resulting transformations of Bakundu way of life namely its values, belief systems and institutions. These complex changes with their contradictions and ambiguities are summed up by the concept of modernization. All of these kindled my desire to publish my findings. It is my belief that this work throws more light on the process of transformation still taking place among the Bakundu and their neighbours.

I relied on my stubborn courage to undertake this work. I should add, however, that I owe sincere thanks to many people for their various contributions. Chief among them is my supervisor, Professor Lovett Z. Elango, who instilled in me the confidence and courage to persevere. His meticulous judgement of facts and his knowledge of the Bakundu culture strengthened my resolve and when I seemed to falter he cheered me on. His rich personal library which I used extensively made my research easier than I ever thought. I thank him immensely for his help and inspiration.

I thank Dr. Mrs. Dorothy Njeuma, former Vice Chancellor of the University of Buea, who at a difficult period in my professional life restored my hope by offering me a position in the University. To Professor Victor Julius Ngoh, I owe a debt of gratitude for sparing time to read through the drafts, for his constructive criticisms, and for his affection and encouragement to continue with hope. I must also thank Professors Nalova Lyonga and Joyce Endeley whose encouraging words and support in all forms reminded me of the duty I owe my people. I cannot forget to thank the late Dr. Herbert Endeley, Professor Albert Azeyeh, the then Dean of the Faculty of Arts and Professor Vincent P. K. Titanji, the then Vice-Chancellor of the University of Buea for the financial support they gave me for my field work.

I also record my thanks to Dr. Canute A. Ngwa and Dr. Timothy Mbuagbo who read and corrected portions of this work. My thanks also go to Dr. Elvira Meoto, Doreen Mekunda and Dr. George Nyamndi for corrections in my language. My colleagues of the Department of History and my students are also remembered for their encouragement.

I thank my entire family, particularly my wife, Patience Ebune and our children who stood firmly by me for sacrificing the pleasures of family life to see me succeed. To Mr. and Dr. Mrs. Sumbele and Mr. and Mrs. George Ngwane, I will always be grateful for being a part of this effort. I also thank Robert Njilla Mengnjo of Bobdan Ventures for his meticulous professionalism in typing this work. I alone, however, am responsible for all errors and flaws in the work.

LIST OF MAPS

Map 1: Location of Bakunduland in Cameroon 19
Map 2: The South West Region Showing
          Bakunduland and other ethnic groups...................20
Map 3: Bakundu migration from Beboka 24
Map 4: The Ethnic Map of the Bakundu 26

LIST OF TABLES

Table 1: Northern Bakundu Villages 31
Table 2: Southern Bakundu Villages 31
Table 3: Population Figures for the Bakundu in 1922...35
Table 4: Livestock in Bakunduland, 1922. 40
Table 5: Bakundu Slave Census by village, 1922..............45
Table 6: Prominent Bakundu families under Colonial Rule. 50
Table 7: Admission fees into Bakundu secret societies 58
Table 7: Plantation Workers from Bakunduland, 1902 – 1906..81
Table 8: Cocoa Farming in Bakundu Villages in 1930...84
Table 9: Bakundu oven census, 1940s and 1950s..............90
Table 10: German Trade Statistics in Bakunduland in 1913 – 1914.......................................91
Table 11: Foodstuff and livestock prices under British rule..94
Table 12: Modern houses in Bakunduland in the 1950s and 1960s.......................................96
Table 13: The Primary School Timetable as Prescribed by the German Education law in 1910...110
Table 14: School attendance in selected Bakundu Villages, 1922 to 1926. 118
Table 15: Number of converts in Bakundu Area in 1898..141

LIST OF ABBREVIATIONS

A.F.C	African Fruit Company
B.C.D.U.	Bakundu Cultural and Development Union
B.S.A.	Bakundu Students' Association
C.D.C	Cameroon Development Corporation
C.P.N.C.	Cameroon People's National Congress
G.C.E.	General Certificate of Education
K.N.C.	Kamerun National Congress
K.P.P.	Kamerun People's Party
N.A.	Native Authority
O.B.E.	Order of the British Empire
U.A.C.	United African Company
U.N.	United Nations

TABLE OF CONTENTS

Preface i
List of maps...ixv
List of tables v
List of abbreviations vi

INTRODUCTION 11

CHAPTER ONE: THE LAND AND THE PEOPLE 17
Introduction 17
The Land 17
Drainage 21
The People...22
Demographics: Population Size, Number of Villages, ...23
Traditional Socio-Political Organisation 31
Settlement Pattern: Villages..31
Demography 34
Traditional Economy...35
Social Hierarchy and Class Structure 40
Succession and Inheritance 48
Politics and Government...51
Conclusion 63

CHAPTER TWO: THE COLONIAL SITUATION 66
Introduction 66
The German Period 66
British Rule 72
German Economic Policy 78
British Economic Policy 82
The Emergence of Cooperative Movements.....................85

Petty Trade and Export Trade 90
The British Phase 94
Conclusion 98

CHAPTER THREE: CHRISTIANITY IN BAKUNDULAND 101
Introduction 101
Missionary Explorations, 1873 – 1875 101
Opening of Bombe Station... 102
Traditional Healers... 103
Agriculture 106
Missionary Schooling 108
Vernacular Schools 111
"German Schools"... 112
Nathaniel Malomba Bebe... 114
Education Under British Rule 117
Evangelism and Conversion 123
Bakundu Converts.. 126
Role of Bakundu Catechists in Evangelisation 129
Effects of the 1914 War 133
Marriage, Family and Society 142
Women in Bakundu Society 144
Conclusion 148

CHAPTER FOUR: NEW SOCIAL FORMS, AGENCIES AND ORIENTATIONS 151
Introduction 151
Education and Modernisation 151
The New Class 153
Bakundu and National Politics....................................... 160

Trade and Business 164
Forms of Marriage 167
Bakundu Improvement Union.. 169
Bakundu Plantation Experience 176
War Veterans... 177
Conclusion 178

CHAPTER FIVE: FROM VILLAGERS TO TOWNSMEN 180
Introduction 180
Urbanism 180
Cooperatives... 183
The Produce Marketing Board 184
Land Speculation... 187
Land and Labour 192
Conclusion 198

GENERAL CONCLUSION 199

BIBLIOGRAPHY 204

INTRODUCTION

The Bakundu people are one of many Bantu groups in the Republic of Cameroon. Located in the immediate hinterland of the Cameroon coast, they, like their neighbours, especially the Duala of the Wouri River, were among the first Cameroonians to have relatively sustained contacts with Europeans and European culture, beginning with the seventeenth Century trans-Atlantic slave trade and continuing with "legitimate commerce" in the nineteenth century. These contacts were initially indirect and there is some evidence that they may have begun in the seventeenth century when an important trade route linking the coastal trading centres of Rio-del-Rey penetrated to Bakunduland. By the nineteenth century, however, these contacts had become relatively more direct and more intense.

Traders were therefore the first Europeans to establish contacts and interact with Bakundu and other coastal Cameroonians. These contacts introduced pre-colonial Cameroonians including Bakundu, to European trade, culture, and thus to westernisation in general which with time contributed to strong and expanding trade and economic ties that became irreversible by the colonial era. More importantly, these commercial contacts and ties were accompanied by less tangible but more revolutionary European cultural influences, both religious and secular, which the Bakundu initially resisted. Eventually, however, when European conquest led to colonial rule and European political domination, the Bakundu recognised the futility of further resistance and accommodated themselves to their new status as subjects of the new rulers.

For the Bakundu, therefore, the coming of Europeans and European colonial rule opened a new chapter in their social and cultural experiences which involved a double but complementary process. First, they protected or tried to protect their traditional ways from the challenge of European ways, a struggle which sometimes pitted them against Christian missionaries and colonial authorities and traders simultaneously. Second, they adopted and adapted those European ways, ideas and techniques which they found unthreatening and useful. Thus, through innovation and adaptation the Bakundu were able to conserve some of their core social values and ancestral ways. In the process, by choice or by force of circumstances, they neither adopted modern European ways wholesale and uncritically nor abandoned wholesale their traditional culture. Both way, these choices were rational and the process continued.

The central problem of this study is to show how the Bakundu responded to the particular challenges and seized opportunities created by the European presence, especially under colonial rule. It examines the dynamics of these multiple and multi-dimensional transformations and is therefore a study of the enduring tension between tradition and modernity, the limits it imposes and the breadth and depth of transformation of Bakundu society. In sum then, it shows how, for example, the Bakundu accepted new farming methods and crops without abandoning traditional peasant farming and crops; how they embraced Western education and economic forms while resisting teachings by Europeans against old forms and modes of thought like witchcraft and polygamous marriages which were integral to their ancestral ways. However reluctantly, this process involved choices, innovation and adaptation, and it continues under the Cameroon national experience. Its end products are a new Bakundu elite, a new Bakundu society and a living, ever-changing Bakundu culture. Essentially, it is a study in culture and change.

Furthermore, the study identifies and describes traditional Bakundu institutions that were most deeply implicated in these transformations and therefore determined the limits of modernisation in Bakundu society. It analyses the dynamics of the cultural transformations in terms of their modernising impact on the Bakundu individual and collective behaviour. Finally, it examines the extent to which the Bakundu domesticated and internalised new European ideas, techniques, forms of behaviour and, contrary to what was once assumed about the nature of the European-African encounter, became the initiators of change rather than simple unwilling victims of the change imposed on them.

Finally, this work undertakes a description of Bakundu urban experience which was closely linked with the new modern agro-economy in which plantations, cooperatives, petty trade and other business forms figured prominently and provided new opportunities for individual wealth and enrichment. Ultimately, it shows how all of these factors together changed Bakundu life ways and how tradition and modernity, far from being mutually incompatible, are ultimately a result of a single but complex process involving continuity and change, innovation and adaptation.

The problem of culture in the modern world has reached a new stage with emerging globalisation whose meaning and implications for the world are not yet fully understood. This makes the study of cultures a very urgent matter and raises the question whether cultures like that of the Bakundu, often considered "primitive" and unprogressive, are destined to disappear in the face of the "clash of civilisations and culture wars" recently dramatized by the growing tensions between Islam and the West, for example[1]

This study is a contribution to the knowledge and understanding necessary for mutual tolerance and

---

[1] See Samuel P. Huntington. *The Clash of Civilisations and The Remaking of World Order*, (A Touchstone Book, New York, 1997).

accommodation among the world's different traditions, great and small. To this end, the word tradition is used here to denote what Vansina calls "a very old and yet dynamic heritage of a complex of worldview and behaviour", something comparable to the use of tradition in expressions like "Judeo-Christian tradition" or "Confucian tradition".[2] This point needs to be emphasised because ultimately, as Vansina reminds us, such traditions are called "civilisation".[3] Thus, the study of the culture history of the Bakundu is essentially and ultimately a study of civilisation.

It is difficult to establish precise time limits for the beginning and the end of this study for two main reasons. First, it covers a long period that roughly begins in c. 1898 with the first recorded Bakundu converts. Second, and more important, it involves processes of change whose remote causes and long-term consequences are too subtle and complex to be fully explained or understood within rigid chronological limits. Ideas, innovations and trends do not appear or disappear abruptly. They tend to overlap each other through time and allowances must be made for the shades of change due to this overlap. Such is the nature of culture history. The study has therefore adopted a chronology that begins c. 1884 and ends with the post-independence era, when the Bakundu became actively involved in modern national politics. In principle, this meant that Cameroon's ethnic diversity would henceforth be managed in a new political framework with potentially greater possibility of inter-ethnic contacts. Bakundu inclusion in the new political order implied that they and other peoples would now compete and thrive in public life more secure in their cultural and social identity. Under colonial rule, the Bakundu, like their neighbours, were politically awakened by the post war

---

[2] Jan Vansina, *Living With Africa*, (Madison: University of Wisconsin Press, 1994), 230.
[3] Ibid.

nationalist ferment which swept across Africa. This ferment led to the formation of the Bakundu Improvement Union by the Bakundu in urban centres. Thus aroused, they participated in national politics, becoming members of political groups or cultural associations, and in the post-independence era politics. This explains why the study ends in 2002, the year in which the Bakundu participation in national politics became most manifest.

Material for this study has been gathered from a variety of sources, primary and secondary. These are of different values and are measured in terms of their strength in interpreting the Bakundu experience under European rule. The archival materials include Intelligence, Assessment and Reassessment reports in the National Archives Buea. Oral testimonies were also collected and despite their limitations, they provided useful information about migration, settlement and resettlement of the Bakundu people. Secondary sources included books, journals, unpublished essays, theses and dissertations. This literature provides some of the theoretical insights of sociology, social and political anthropology that have been used in this work. In all these works the Bakundu have just been mentioned. There is no full-length study devoted to the Bakundu, their society and their culture history. This study attempts to fill this gap and to contribute to Cameroon historiography, specifically and to Bantu historiography generally.

This work is divided into five chapters with an introduction and a conclusion. Chapter One describes the land and the people. Chapter Two reviews the colonial situation, laying emphasis on the German and British administrations. Chapter Three is devoted to the discussion of Christianity in Bakunduland and concludes with a summary of continuity and change between traditional and European ideas and institutions. Chapter Four discusses new social forms, agencies and orientations and Chapter Five looks at the Bakundu from villagers to townsmen. The General Conclusion summarises and interprets the whole work in the light of the study of culture, culture change and modernisation.

CHAPTER ONE
THE LAND AND THE PEOPLE

Introduction

Bakunduland, the home of the Bakundu people of the Republic of Cameroon, lies in the equatorial region between latitudes 2° and 13° north of the equator and longitudes 8° and 16° east and has two distinct seasons a dry season and a rainy season. The rainy season lasts for eight months from March to October and the dry season from November to February. Average annual rainfall is 4000mm and average daily temperature is 20°C. These climatic conditions create a tropical climate of high temperatures averaging 20°C and high humidity averaging 70%. This combination of heavy rainfall, high daily temperatures and high humidity results in a climate that favours luxuriant flora and fauna,[4] and, not least, a variety of disease-bearing insect pests, especially a variety of mosquitoes, vectors of debilitating malaria. Together, these factors result in a tropical ecology that dictates the nature, variety and rhythm of human activity, notably agriculture.

The Land

Bakunduland is divided into two more or less distinct zones. Northern Bakundu, is located in north-western Meme Division, previously Kumba Division. This zone lies between longitudes $9^014`$ and $9^028`$ east of the Greenwich Meridian and between latitudes $4^055`$ and $5^061`$ north of the equator.[5] It has a surface area of about 240 square kilometres[6]. Much of Northern Bakunduland is hilly and

---

[4] Aaron Suh Neba. *Modern Geography of the Republic of Cameroon* 2nd Edition (New York: Neba Publishers, 1987), 24.
[5] A. D. Garson "Reassessment Report on the Bakundu Tribal Area, Kumba Division". File No. AC 61 /143/1 vol. 1932. National Archives Buea. Henceforth NAB.
[6] Ibid.

reaches a high altitude of 1150m as one travels from south to north, except for a low lying enclave between the villages of Wone and Ibemi.[7] The eastern part of this zone is marked by steep valleys where streams forming the headwaters of the River Mungo rise.

Southern Bakundu has a surface area of some 240km^2, and is located between longitude $9^0 12`$ and $9^0 28`$ and latitude $4^0 23`$ and $4^0 28`$ north of the Equator.[8] In contrast with the north it is low lying. It has an average height between 50 and 350m above sea level, and the land is more fertile and easier to farm. As a result, farms are larger and have higher yields. Travel and transportation of goods and the flow of information are relatively easy. The area is bordered to the north by the Mbonge and Barombi ethnic groups; to the west and east by the Balong, and to the south by the Bakweri.

Soil types in Bakunduland vary with the locality. A greater part of northern Bakundu has volcanic soils while plutonic rocks are found in patches all over the land.[9] Much of northern Bakundu experiences soil erosion although in general, the soils support tropical crops. Patches of old sedimentary rock are found in the valleys of the Mungo River south of Konye and most of Southern Bakundu. Despite problems of leaching and erosion in northern Bakundu the soils are fertile in places, support a variety of tropical food crops like plantains, the staple diet of the Bakundu, yams, cassava, cocoyams and bananas, vegetables as well as cash crops, mainly cocoa, rubber, coffee and oil palm.

---

[7] Nyenti Napoleon Ambi "Bakundu Culture History: A Background Study (Post Graduate Diploma Dissertation in History, University of Yaounde, 1990), 3.
[8] Cyril Elad Eparh "The Balkanisation of the Bakundu from Pre-colonial to 1922: A Study in Underdevelopment (M.A. Thesis in History, University of Yaounde 1, 2005), 13.
[9] Ejedepang-Koge cited by Cyril Elad Eparh "The Balkanisation of the Bakundu from Pre-colonial to 1922: A Study in Underdevelopment" (M.A. Thesis in History, University of Yaounde I, 2005), 16.

Map 1: Location of Bakunduland in Cameroon

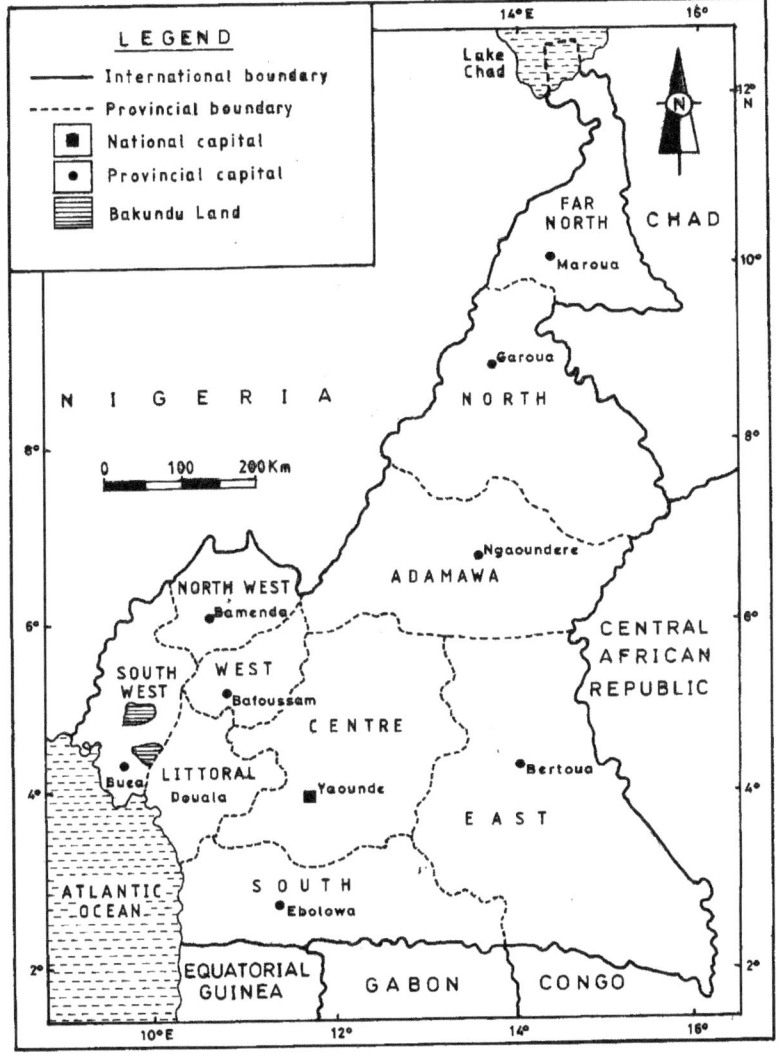

Source: Adapted from the Atlas of the United Republic of Cameroon (Paris: Edition Jeune Afrique, 1980).

Map 2: The South West Region Showing Bakunduland and other ethnic groups

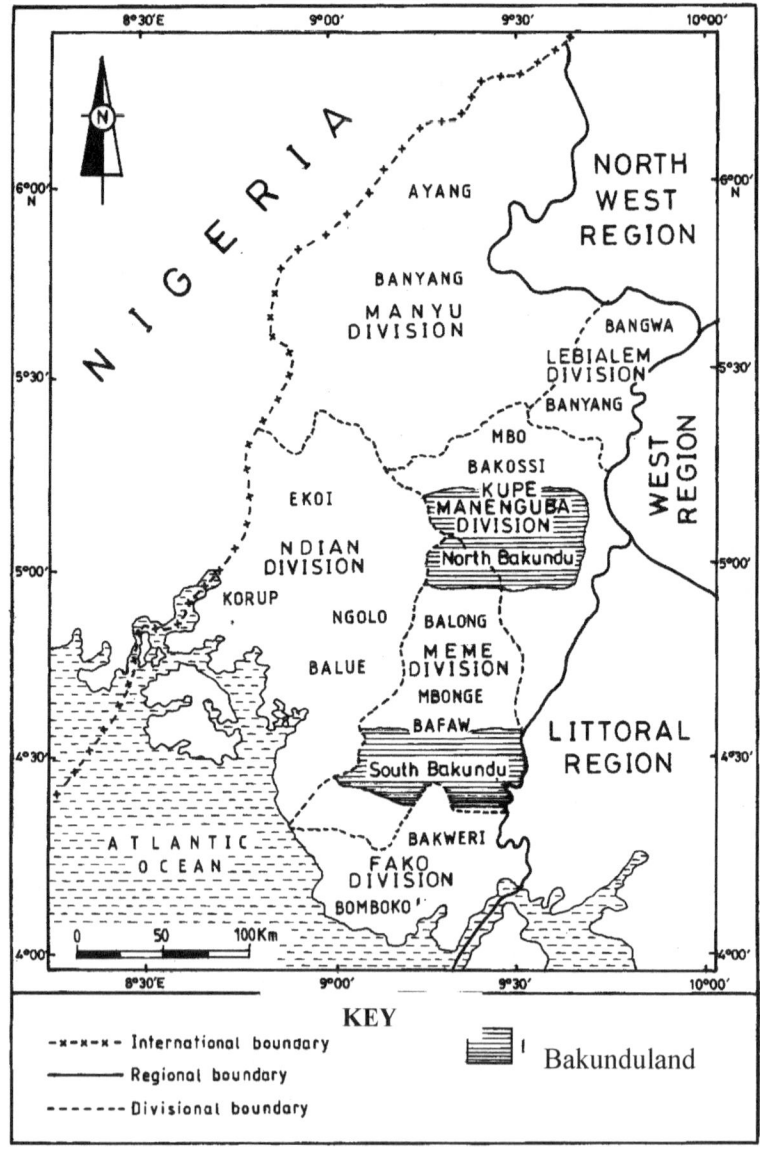

Drainage

The main rivers are the Mungo and the Meme which rise from the Rumpi Hills and drain into the Atlantic Ocean. These rivers flow along the east and western boundaries of Bakunduland respectively and provide limited navigation by dugout canoes. During pre-colonial periods, Bombe in the south was an inland river port on the Mungo and several neighbouring villages like Banga commercially benefited from this river. Traders from Douala area used the Mungo River to transport their goods to Bombe. From Bombe, the goods were carried by porters to villages within the region. On the other hand, cocoa, palm produce, rubber and food crops were shipped to European traders along the coast on River Mungo. Similarly, the Meme River in the west was the main outlet to the Atlantic coast. The Bakundu and Mbonge transported their products to the Atlantic coast through the Meme and received European products through it. It served mainly the Bakundu villages of Boa, Nake, Foe, Ngongo, Bole and Pete.

Bakunduland in general is covered by equatorial forest, almost all of which is virgin. In the south, however, farming and lumbering have led to considerable deforestation. Before this, the area was rich in trees of economic value like mahogany and obeche, and wildlife, different bird species and a variety of medicinal plants and nutritional fruits. Around Mbu is the Korup National Park[10] which marks the boundary with Balue country bordering Bakunduland in the north. This park was created in 1936 by the British colonial government. In July 2004, by Presidential Decree No. 2004/192, the Native Authority Reserve was renamed Korup National Park in order to protect the rare plant and animal species found in it. It covers an area of 326

---

[10] A. D. Garson "Reassessment Report on the Bakundu Tribal Area, Kumba Division". File No. AC61/143/1 Vol. 1932. NAB.

square miles and consists of all the land from all Korup villages in Ndian Division stretching as far as Calabar in Nigeria, and a large proportion of Balundu villages. Its northerly limit extends to the Meme-Manyu Divisional boundary and eastwards the boundary is the Ikenge-Bajaw path.[11]

The Korup forest is one of the few tropical rain forests in the world which has suffered relatively little from human activity. Its resources are still largely unexploited. To preserve this ecosystem villages like Ekondokondo located within the Park are being relocated and provided with amenities like schools and health centres. The park is home to a variety of flora and fauna which have been exploited in traditional ways. Thus, the physical geography of Bakunduland has provided the people a habitat with many advantages which determines their settlement pattern and life style. The negative effects of disease-bearing insects continue to be a problem to the people, however.

The People
The word Bakundu is the plural form of *Kundu,* its singular form in *Lokundu*, a language spoken by the Bakundu. The word itself means *secret.* To understand Bakundu culture and society, one must also understand the cultures of their neighbours and kinsmen from whom they have borrowed much and to whom they have also given much. For the purpose of this study, the closest of these kinsmen and neighbours are the Mbonge, Balue, Ngolo and Balundu who together with the Bakundu are commonly called *Orocko*[12], as well as Bafo, Balong and Bakossi.

---

[11] File No. 13236 Qh/C/1936/3 Korup Native Administration Forest Reserve, Kumba Division, Cameroons Province.
[12] The word "*Orocko*" means welcome in their different languages.

Demographics: Population Size, Number of Villages,
The origin, settlement and resettlement of the Bakundu are discussed here somewhat more extensively for two reasons. First, the Bakundu and their neighbours have lived in close proximity over generations and have borrowed culturally from and intermarried with each other. Second, and more important for the purpose of this study, some of the more important changes in Bakundu society have been brought about by contact with some of their neighbours through economic activities like trading. The traditions of origin of the Bakundu, Bakossi, Bafo, Balong as well as the Bassossi and Mbonge have one thing in common: an eponymous ancestor variously known as Ngoeh, Ngoe or Ngoh. According to these traditions, the founding father of the Bakundu was Ngoe who had two sons, Mauma and Mukundu. It is not certain who Ngoe was. He seems to have been different from the Bakossi Ngoe because they had different cradlelands. The Bakundu cradleland was Beboka in present-day Ndian Division while the Bakossi Ngoe was in Kupe-Manenguba in Bakossiland. Distance however may not have been a problem because ideas, techniques and traits of material and spiritual culture travelled or were diffused over long distances across the continent of Africa. Mauma and Mukundu legend suggest that they once lived together at Beboka. But they quarrelled over farmland and this led to their separation. Mukundu's children came to be known as Bakundu in Meme Division and Mauma's were called Bauma and Bima, now found in present-day Ndian Division. Regarding migration, traditions say the Bakundu migrated from Bekoka.

Map 3: Bakundu migration from Beboka

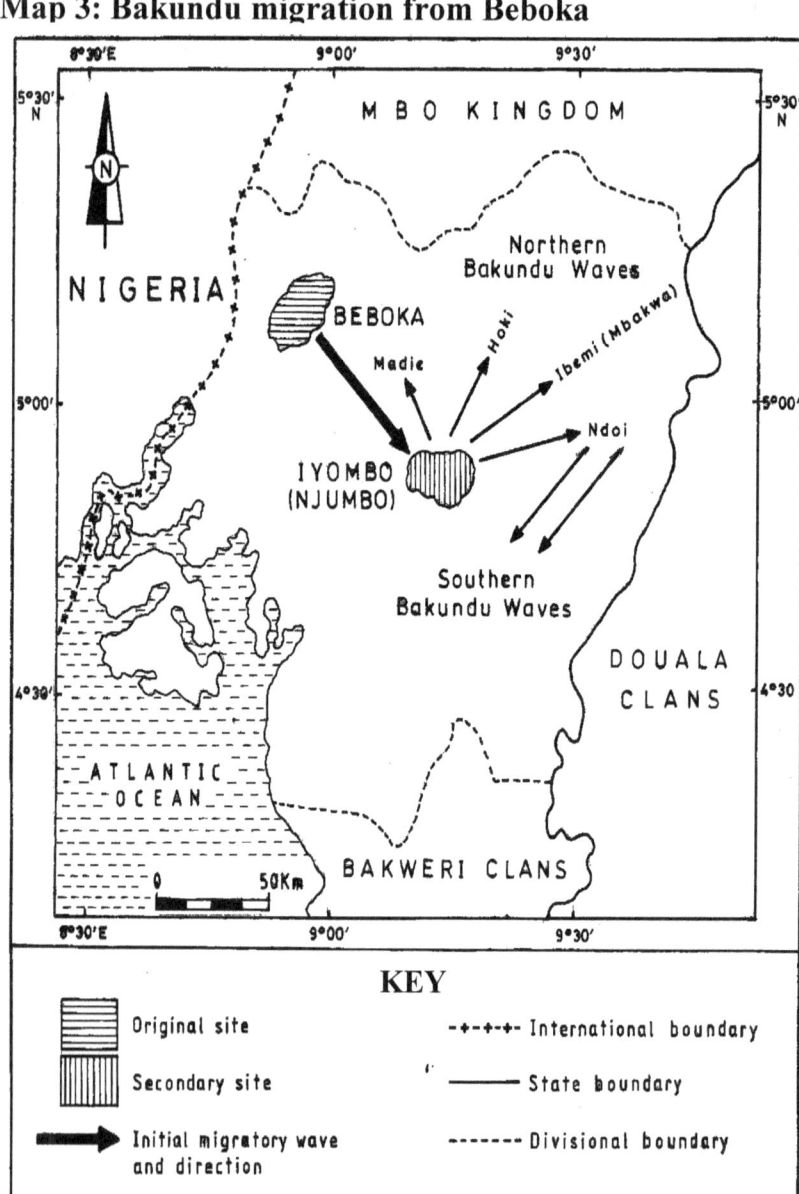

Source: Napoleon Nyenti Ambi "Bakundu Culture History A Background Study" (Post Graduate Diploma Dissertation) University of Yaounde, 1990, P. 17

They founded a new settlement at Iyombo, north of Kita Balue. At Iyombo, the Bakundu quarrelled with the Balue, Mbonge and Balundu peoples over hunting grounds and farmland. These disagreements forced them to leave Iyombo.[13] The migration from Iyombo brought about the dispersal of the Bakundu in different directions. Some families moved eastwards where villages like Konye and Ndoi were founded while others went southwards and founded villages like Bombe, Banga and Pete among others.

Those who went eastwards passed through Madie Ngolo and crossed the Madie River to establish four new villages: Ibemi Nayoh, Itoki, Konye and Ndoi. The families which went southwards settled at Ngongo, Foe, Boa, Bole and Nake. These migrations led the Bakundu to split and formed the northern and southern Bakundu which subsequently developed semi-independently of each other.[14]

Another version of the Bakundu myth of origins is provided by A. D. Garson who has investigated the possible link between the Bakundu and the Bakossi, who also claim Ngoe as their ancestor. In this version, there was a great war between two Bakossi clans, the Elung and Ninong. The Elung could not resist the might of the Ninong. To win the war, the Elung contacted the wise men of Bakundu. The Bakundu elders asked them what kind of ammunition they were using. The Elung revealed that they were using wild cana seeds. Cana seeds were not as hard as shards of ceramic, so when shot at the enemy could not penetrate the body like ceramic. The Bakundu elders advised the Elung to use shards of ceramic pots. Armed with this weapon, the Elung defeated the Ninong. In a celebration to mark their victory the Elung invited the Bakundu elders and vowed to call themselves the

---

[13] File No. 143/1631 Vol. 2. Reassessment Report of the Bakundu Clan in Kumba Division. NAB.
[14] Ibid.

sons of Ngoe as a sign of gratitude to the Bakundu.[15] Elsewhere in the account, Garson claims that any war in which the Bakundu were involved resulted in further migration of the Bakundu to a new settlement.

Map 4: The Ethnic Map of the Bakundu

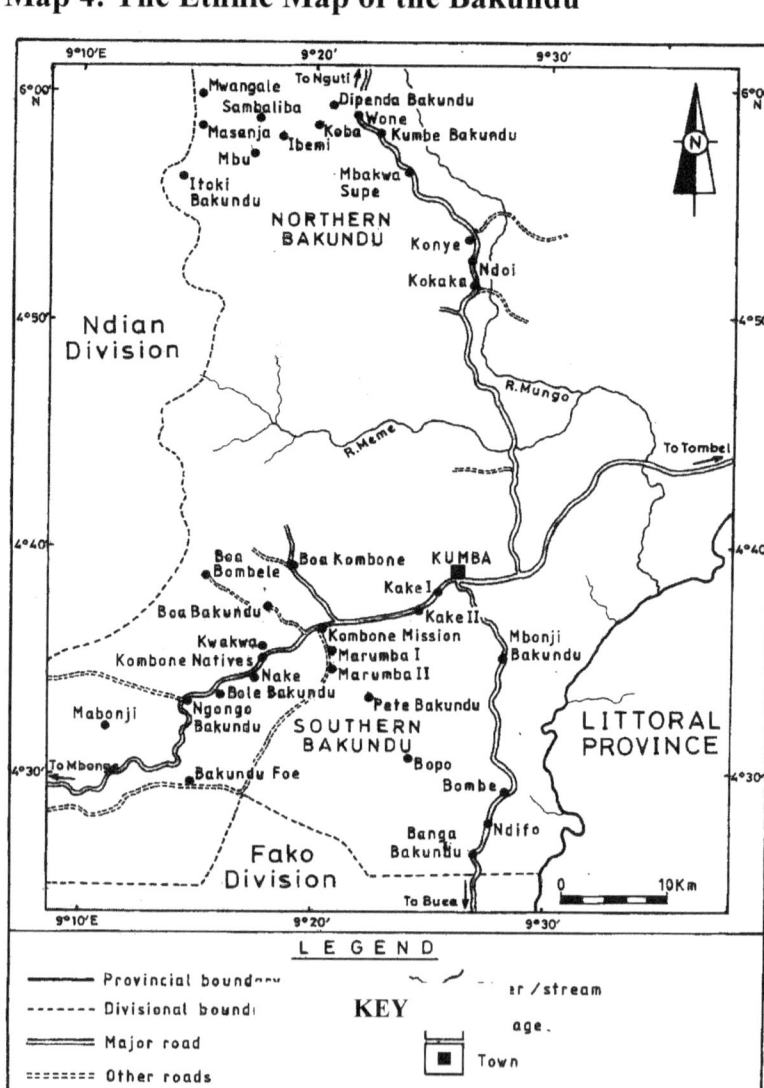

[15] Ibid.

This "mystical" account of the Elung-Ninong war cannot be verified but it suggests that ceramic technology was part of Bakundu culture and provided them certain advantages over their neighbours. What those advantages may have been must remain a mystery for now. In any case, it suggests that the Bakundu were already masters in the art of war which is why they knew which ammunition to use to defeat the enemy. The Elung used broken pieces of ceramic pots suggesting that the Bakundu may also have used them to defeat their enemies. Garson may have mistaken skirmishes between the Bakundu and their neighbours for wars. However, oral tradition holds that they were many skirmishes over land not wars in the conventional sense. These varying interpretations notwithstanding, the question of war cannot be completely ruled out if by war we mean organised violence, regardless of how large or small the scale of hostilities. From this perspective, it seems that the conflicts might have been wars in every sense of the term. After all, they were, like modern wars, about vital interests: land, fishing and hunting rights, the simple technologies used notwithstanding. Besides, the ethnic groups used their strategic weapons like witchcraft and other "magical" arts to achieve their objectives.

Another ethnic group which shares the same ancestor with the Bakundu are the Bafo. Bafo tradition holds that Ngoh was their genitor-ancestor. Some oral sources say that the Bafo first settled at Nsambia and Masui in the Mbo plain of the modern Western Region of Cameroon.[16] From there they moved southwards and encountered the Bakossi with whom they clashed over land, fishing and hunting grounds. At this stage, the Bakossi like the Bafo were still migrating to their ultimate, perhaps unknown destination. These migrations were therefore largely disorderly and followed no particular logic except, as in the case of Bafo, the desire to

---

[16] Ibid.

make trade contact with the Whiteman at the coast. The encounter between the Bafo and Bakossi led to a bloody war with considerable loss of life on both sides. After the war and following the continuous tensions between them, the Bafo crossed the Mungo River and established themselves at Kokobuma, Dikome, Kombone and Kurume[17] along the modern Kumba-Mamfe trunk road. Henceforth, they shared boundaries with the Bakundu with whom they lived peacefully. It is from these settlements that they moved southwards and founded other Bafo villages. The Bafo migrations, it must be noted, were motivated by their quest for a share in the lucrative European trade that was then expanding and acted as a distant magnet for them and other groups.

The Bakundu, Bafo and Bakossi are thus descendants of a single eponymous ancestor variously known as Ngoh or Ngoe. The traditions of the Bakossi claim that the founder of the Bakossi ethnic group was a man called Ngoe who was different from the Bakundu Ngoe as already noted. It is believed that Ninong was the site of dispersal and migration.[18] Ngoe lived at Mwekan in Upper Bakossi around the Kupe-Manenguba Mountain and was a hunter. On one of his hunting expeditions he met a woman, Sumediang, whom he married and with whom he had seven sons who founded the seven Bakossi clans.

The traditions of origin of the Balong are, like those of the groups already cited, obscure. They also claim Ngoe as their ancestral father. They claim that the group originated from Menge River, just north of modern Ikiliwindi in Meme Division. From here, led by Ekoko, the group moved south to found the village of Boa. From Boa, they split and one

---

[17] R.W.M. Dundas and F.B. Carr Reassessment Report on the Bafaw, Kumba Division, Cameroon Province, NAB.
[18]

group migrated further south and settled close to the Bafo in Meme Division. Further migrations culminated in the creation of Mukonje, Mundame, Malende, Muyuka and other villages.[19] The main motive for migrations seems to have been the search for trading opportunities. The Balong migrations do not seem to have been peaceful in the main.

All these people are Bantus. Edwin Ardener classifies them as belonging to the north-westerly branch of the Bantu-speaking people consisting of two major clusters of considerable size and geographical extent.[20] All the groups have traditions of migration from elsewhere and different starting points. If these traditions are to be believed, it means that they are linked, first and foremost, by common genealogical ties eventually traced to the semi-mythical Ngoe or Ngoh. Living as they did in close proximity, these genealogical ties have been reinforced by inter marriage, common economic interests and extensive cultural borrowing, hence the conflation of the Ngoe or Ngoh myth.

The movement of the Bakundu towards the south from Beboka was without major conflict. No doubt, there were skirmishes, but this does not seem to have led to major wars as Paul Akama Eseme notes:

> The movements were generally peaceful and where there were some troubles, our forefathers fought hard to avoid war because they knew our people would always live together. Besides, the fact that our people got married to women from other ethnic groups as they themselves did to Bafo women was enough to make our people to avoid war. This explains why even today such clashes over land

---

[19] F.B. Carr Reassessment Report on the Balong Tribal Area of Kumba Division, Cameroon Province, NAB.
[20] Edwin Ardener, *Coastal Bantu of the Cameroon* (London: International African Institute, 1956), 10.

have been handled with a lot of care. Rather than fight each other few of such cases have been brought before the law courts.[21]

There were no wars as the account above shows because the Bakundu and their neighbours preferred to live with each other in peace. The peace that reigns in Bakunduland has even in modern times contributed in making Bakunduland a haven for people from other regions of this country. It is this fact that led Andrew Kemba Mosongo to note that:

> They did not form a homogeneous group (geographically) since you can find Bafo, Balong, Mbonge, and Bakossi villages in the same geographical area. They are therefore a peace loving people, dynamic in the cultivation of their land, and very accommodative. For almost half a century that I have lived on this planet, I have never heard or seen Bakundu people quarrelling with their neighbours and no history teacher has ever taught me anything about inter-tribal wars between the Bakundu, Barombi, Balong or any other ethnic group with which the Bakundu inhabit, so to speak, the Kumba central sub-division in particular, the Meme Division in general. On the contrary, from my primary school days, I have always been told and I am convinced, that we are kinsmen to the Bakossi, Bassossi, Mbo, Barombi, Bafo etc.[22]

---

[21] Conversation with Akama Eseme at Kumba on 17 March 2006. Mr. Eseme is a Bafo notable and a member of the Bafo traditional council in Kumba. He is 89.

[22] A. K. Mosongo, "A keynote address presented by the Congress Bureau of the Bakundu Cultural and Development Meeting on the occasion of their 14th Annual Gathering at Bole – Dipenda on the 18th of January 1987". He is a Bakundu elite and Director of Linguistic Centre, Buea. Aged 76.

Mosongo's statement is worthy of extended comment. It says something about Bakundu ethos: They were/are a people who live peacefully with their neighbours and explains why so many people from different regions of the country live among them as noted already.

These statements tend to preclude the idea that the movement by the Bakundu and eventual settlement in the north and south resulted in wars between the Bakundu and their neighbours, although this is not very clear because further research may refute this argument and show proof that these wars were actually fought.

Traditional Socio-Political Organisation
Settlement Pattern: Villages

In the northern and southern clusters the village is the basic socio-political unit of Bakundu. A village comprised many lineages each headed by a lineage head, usually the oldest man or patriarch. Tables 1 and 2 respectively show northern and southern Bakundu villages.

Table 1: Northern Bakundu Villages

Itoki	Sambaliba	Wone
Muangale	Koba	Kumbe
Mosanja	Dipenda	Mbakwa Supe
Mbu	Masaka	Konye
Ibemi	Kokaka	Ndoi

Source: Hansley Nagweya Ewane, "The Bakundu Cultural and Development Meeting (BCDM) 1975-2000: An Historical Analysis". B.A. Long Essay, University of Buea, 2005.

Table 2: Southern Bakundu Villages

Kake I	Bole I	Boa
Kake II	Bole II	Marumba I
Kombone Miso	Ngongo	Marubma II

Kombone Town	Mabonji	Ngonge
Kwa Kwa	Bopo	Bombe
Nake I	Pete	Banga I
Nake II	Foe	Banga II

Source: Hansley Nagweya Ewane, "The Bakundu Cultural and Development Meeting (BCDM) 1975-2000: An Historical Analysis". B.A. Long Essay, University of Buea, 2005.

Villages like Mwangale, Mosanja and Sambaliba are newly-created villages which splintered from Itoki and Ibemi, the parent villages in the late 1930s. This pattern of constant fragmentation reflects the characteristic binary fission of the Bantu which has been widely noted by scholars. It reflects the "fragmentation" of maximal lineages when a group becomes too large and natural resources become scarce. To avoid tensions and conflicts the younger branch of the lineage usually migrates and founds a village at a new site not far from the parent community. This "law" or practice accounts for the Bakundu conflict with the Balue, Mbonge, Balundu over hunting grounds and farmlands, which forced Bakundu to leave Iyombo, as mentioned earlier, and provides some indirect evidence of this process.

All villages were built in a linear form with houses facing each other as a sign of belonging and a way of peaceful co-existence. At the centre of each village was a building called *etana* or town hall where decisions affecting the village were made. It is, so to speak, the heart of politics and government. Women, slaves and strangers were not admitted into it because it was a meeting place for male secret societies. This institution no longer exists. In most Bakundu villages, it has been transformed into an assembly hall; it can now be found only in the villages of Mbu and Itoki. Modern community halls have replaced them, a sign of modernity. These assembly halls are built using modern building materials like cement and zinc and are large in size unlike the *etana* which was built out of local materials like mud, sticks and thatches. This change is partly due to population growth which led to the creation of modern wards and streets. Taking advantage of this change, many wealthy Bakundu, like Chief Rudolf Duala Itoe of Bombe in Southern Bakundu and Chief David Besingi of Ibemi, to name only two, moved their homes away from the older, congested sections of their villages to enjoy some privacy.

Chief Rudolf Duala Itoe
A Civil Administrator and Modern Bakundu Chief

Bakundu villages were dispersed settlements for two main reasons: the desire for more land for farming and the control of trade routes. In Bakunduland the prominent trade centres were Bombe along the banks of the Mungo River and Ngongo on the banks of the Meme River, all in Southern

Bakundu. Others included Bole and Banga. These villages had market places where buyers and sellers met every seven days.[23] It is noteworthy that the populations of these villages were multi-ethnic; non-indigenes from the grass fields and Igbo from Nigeria were attracted to them by the opportunities to do profitable business. As will be seen in the next chapter the activities of the traders from other ethnic groups were controlled by the Bakundu.

Almost all Bakundu villages were founded by hunters like Netongo of Mbu and Namana of Ibemi[24] are the best known. The two most important factors that determined choice of a village site seem to have been the availability of fertile soil, water and fauna. Thus, it is noteworthy that most Bakundu villages are located at or near large streams or rivers,[25] inside a forest enclave suggesting a deliberate choice of site and habitat with access to natural resources and healthy wholesome environment.

Demography

Lack of records makes it impossible to say exactly what the total population of Bakundu is. However, the population of all Bakundu in 1922 was estimated by R. W. M. Dundas and F. B. Carr as shown in Table 3. It seems reasonable to argue that villages like Ibemi, Mbu, Itoki, Supe, Bombe and Boa existed since the fourteenth century except for the newly-created villages like Mosanja, Mwangale and Sambaliba because of contacts the former had established with the people along the coast. By the fourteenth century the Bakundu were already trading with European traders on the coast on tropical goods like ivory.

---

[23] Bohannan and Curtin, *Africa and Africans*, 109.
[24] Conversation with Chief Nakomo at Kumba on 26 April 2007. Chief of Mbu Village. He is chief of Mbu and aged 81.
[25] Ibid.

Table 3: Population Figures for the Bakundu in 1922.

Sex	No. of People
Males	1532
Females	1906
Boys	1269
Girls	1106
Total	**5,813**

Source: R. W. M. Dundas and F. B. Carr Assessment Report 1922 on the Bakundu and Mbonge Tribes, Kumba Division, Cameroon Province, N. A. B.

The figures in Table 3 are rough estimates at best, compiled by administrators and intended for administrative use. They cannot therefore be taken at face value and there is no independent source to crosscheck them to determine whether the total population of the Bakundu was in fact higher or lower, or what the population density per square mile was, nor is it possible to calculate average village densities. The most that can be said, therefore, is that the Bakundu were and are one of the largest ethnic groups in Meme Division based on the number and size of Bakundu villages. However, there are no comparative figures to confirm this.

Traditional Economy
In all Bakundu villages there are different occupational groups. Prior to the coming of European traders to the Cameroon coast, the Bakundu were agriculturalists growing food staples like cocoyams, plantains and yams. Other food staples included sweet potatoes and cassava, root crops as well as a variety of vegetables like okra and spinach, while grains like corn, groundnuts and upland rice were cultivated in the villages of Kake, Ndoi, Kokaka, Konye, Mbu, Itoki and

Mbakwa Supe.²⁶ In addition to farmers, hunters and fishermen, there were smiths, whose existence is evidence that the Bakundu were familiar with iron metallurgy. The iron hoes, machetes, knives and spearheads used by the Bakundu were thus produced locally. When and how they acquired the skill is uncertain: there is no evidence of iron deposits in Bakunduland so they may have learned it through contact with Eastern Nigerians, possibly, the Igbo. As elsewhere in Africa, smithing in Bakunduland was shrouded in mystery and taboos.²⁷ The mystery surrounding smiths, their occupation and the ubiquity and utility of their products made them a much respected, even feared, social caste.

The Oil palm, (*Elaeius guineensis*), which has many economic uses grew wild on Bakunduland. When ripe the nut was sometimes roasted and eaten but more typically was boiled to extract oil. A European visitor remarked poetically that the oil combined "the odour of violets, a taste approaching our olive, and a colour purer and more perfect than saffron".²⁸ Oil palm was the pioneer export crop early in the nineteenth century, and it was joined by palm kernels and groundnuts in the second half of the century. The fact that these products already grew in West Africa, where they were traded and consumed as foodstuffs, helps to explain why the end of the Atlantic slave trade did not cause a complete disruption of overseas commerce, though it does not mean that the transition was entirely smooth. The expansion of exports of palm products was a response to industrial growth in Europe, which led to a rise in the demand for oils and fats.

---

[26] R W M. Dundas and F. B. Carr Assessment Report on the Bakundu and Mbonge Tribes, Kumba Division, Cameroon Province. NAB.
[27] From an enlightening discussion of the role of smiths in one African society, see Candice L. Goucher, Charles A. LEGuin, Linda A. Walton, *In the Balance Themes in Global History* (Boston, Massachusetts: McGraw Hill, 1998), 236-237.
[28] Robert W. July, *Pre-Colonial Africa: An Economic and Social History* (England: Davidson Publishing Ltd, 1976), 102 – 103.

Palm oil was used in the production of soap, lubricants and candles. Soap was required for cleansing the population in the growing urban centres; lubricants were needed to oil the new machinery, especially the railways; and candles were in demand for lighting the expanding towns and factories.[29]

The economy has generally been described as a subsistence economy although the concept of 'subsistence' is an inadequate characterisation of the Bakundu production system. With the development of agriculture, the Bakundu became a 'colonizing' people, expanding their numbers and their territory through migrations. This could not have occurred if their economy was based merely on subsistence production. To expand and colonise, a society needs to produce surpluses or more than its own immediate needs.[30] African traditional social organization, religious and political life also seem to refute the concept of a subsistence economy.[31] The existence of such a system in which people specialise in various activities suggests the existence of economic diversity which can be used for other purposes.

The oil palm grew wild in the forest. The oil that was produced by traditional methods was consumed locally and formed part of the local diet. As the industrial demand for palm oil grew in the nineteenth century, as it was used as a machine lubricant, the British colonial government adopted policies to promote scientific production. This led Governor Hugh Clifford of Nigeria to declare an embargo against felling oil palms by declaring that "…no person shall for the purpose of manufacturing liquor fell any palm or tap oil palm

---

[29] A.G. Hopkins, *An Economic History of West Africa* (New York: Longman Group Ltd., 1973), 128-129.
[30] J. E. Flint "Economic Change in West Africa in the Nineteenth Century" in J. F. A. Ajayi and Michael Grouder, *History of West Africa Vol.11* (Ibadan: Longman Publishers, 19), 381.
[31] Ibid.

in such a manner as to kill the tree ...".[32] In addition, the colonial government provided subsidies to farmers to discourage the felling of palm trees. Despite these administrative measures, the Bakundu continued to fell palm trees for a variety of uses including palm wine production.

Traditionally, fresh palm wine is an important item for entertainment and hospitality. It is also used in religious rituals. It is known to have a high yeast content. When fermented it produces a local alcoholic beverage, "illicit gin" in colonial legislation, which was traded and consumed locally. The rotten tree trunks provided mushroom that enriched the people's protein needs.

The Bakundu used basic agricultural techniques like rotational bush fallow and shifting cultivation. Fallowing was practised once the crop yield began to decline. The burning of bush cover deposited fertilising ash on the land.[33] Machetes and hoes together made possible the slash-and-burn or swinden agricultural technique, a seasonally-regulated practice for bringing a patch of forest under cultivation. It involved clearing and burning the forest and little or no hoeing, before planting of crops. Shifting cultivation was also common. It involved moving from a piece of land to a new site after a number of years of cultivation when the fertility of the soil was deemed exhausted.[34] This allowed the old piece of land to recover its fertility.

Other aspects of the traditional Bakundu economy included hunting, fishing and gathering. Fresh water fishing by net, line, and harpoon provided vital protein for the people. Hunting and trapping were limited essentially to small game such as porcupines, birds, hares and monkeys.

---

[32] File No. Qc/d 1917/1 Restriction as to palm wine and palm trees, Cameroon Province 1917. NAB.
[33] Flint "Economic Change", 385.
[34] Paul Bohannan and Philip Curtin, *Africa and Africans* Fourth Edition (Illinois: Waveland Press, Inc., 1988), 23-24.

Larger game like elephants which provided ivory, as well as lions were hunted by pit traps which were large holes dug in the ground. When animals fell into them they could not escape.

    The Bakundu were elephant hunters and the ivory from the hunting enabled them to trade with Europeans for luxury goods like mirrors, cloth, tobacco, wines, and iron utensils. Elango, the ivory produced here was flawless unlike that produced from other parts of West Africa.[35]

    Weaving and wood carving were also important activities of the pre-colonial Bakundu economy. Artisans and craftsmen produced bowls, raffia bags, baskets, stools, hoes and cutlasses, all household utensils which were also bartered in local trade. Animal husbandry raised livestock like goats, sheep, short-horned cattle, hogs and poultry for domestic needs and for local trade. Goats, sheep and cattle figured prominently as bride-wealth in marriage transactions and were a standard of value, a measure of prestige and wealth.

---

[35] Elango, *Bimbia*, 71.

Table 4: Livestock in Bakunduland, 1922

Animals	Population
Goats	1,099
Sheep	498
Pig	206
Cattle	139

Source: R. W. M. Dundas and F. B, Carr. Assessment Report. 1922, on the Bakundu and Mbonge Tribes, Kumba Division, Cameroon Province NAB.

As in many other traditional African societies, the Bakundu economy was based on division of labour by gender. Specific farm and household tasks were assigned to men and women. Thus, men did the clearing of the land while women tilled the soil and planted the crops. The men and women shared weeding and harvesting. With this division of labour went a corresponding allocation of land to grow food. Other tasks like clearing new land, roofing houses, or building walls; mending roofs, clearing bush paths or building bridges required collective labour. These were often performed by village associations like age-grades.[36] Specific age-groups or grades were assigned certain duties. All of this required and presupposed a well organised community and family life. In this way, even the family was an economic unit. Because the Bakundu were not autarchic: they depended on the products of other communities and this led to exchange.

Social Hierarchy and Class Structure

Bakundu society was stratified. At the top of the social structure were the titleholders, who were freeborn or *Konja*. They were distinguished by their wealth and/or acts of bravery either in battle or hunting. Below them were the

---

[36] July, *Pre-Colonial Africa*, 109.

"middle class" or wise men whose opinions were always sought because they were wealthy. They had an enviable status in society. At the bottom were the "slaves" *mofa* or *mopa*, persons who were captured in war and sold as slaves. These were not titles but names used to distinguish one group of people from the other.

Bakundu slaves belonged to and worked for their owner. Slaves had no social status and were little respected no matter how hardworking or intelligent they were. They could not own property since they were considered the property of their owner. Nor could slaves achieve elder status, whatever their age. They had no right to an opinion in a court or public discussion, nor could they participate in any traditional rites and ceremonies.[37]

The treatment and status of domestic slaves varied from village to village. War captives from other groups could be sold. Those who were absorbed into the family worked for the master but also for themselves.[38] They often became integrated into the households of their owners and there was little obvious difference between their lifestyle and that of their owners, except that they did not enjoy privileges reserved for free borns.[39]

Slaves did not live in the same compound with their masters. They lived in slave quarters or villages adjacent to the free settlements, a practice which was common in other communities that owned slaves.[40] This residential segregation was the most obvious distinction between them and the freeborn. The children of freeborn were in principle not allowed to visit slave villages nor were the children of slaves allowed to travel freely. The activities of slaves in

---

[37] File No. Ae 37, 1922 Assessment Report on the Tribal Areas of Mbonge and Bakundu, NAB.
[38] Ibid. 94.
[39] Ibid.
[40] Ibid.

these villages were closely monitored. For example, they used the same streams or rivers but could not bathe upstream. They buried their dead without any rituals for fear of being considered rebellious. All these restrictions were repressive and intended to keep them permanently under the control of their masters.[41]

In principle, the Bakundu do not seem to have enslaved other Bakundu or raided other groups specifically for slaves. But the last word cannot be said here about this age-old and widespread institution among the Bakundu. Nevertheless, it is certain that slaves in Bakunduland came from the grassfields and were either kidnapped travellers or war captives or both.[42] In Bakundu social etiquette male slaves could marry freeborn women, but the children of such union belonged to the slave owner who paid the bride-wealth. The children born of such unions were free being filiated to the owner's patrilineage.[43] So their servitude was not without rights. There was no self-redemption of slaves. The phrase *Konja ja Bakundu* (freeborn) Bakundu reflected the fact that a person had no slave ancestry.

Although slaves were integrated into the family of the owner, they laboured under some social stigma and other disabilities. Before the introduction of the trans-Atlantic slave trade a slave, male or female, juvenile or adult, could be put to any kind of work, punished at will or sold.[44] What Oliver says about the African experience with the slave trade applies to the Bakundu to a large extent. When slaves were no longer needed, they were set free without any compensation or sold to those who needed them.

---

[41] Dundas and Carr. Reassessment Report on the Bakundu and Mbonge Tribes, NAB.
[42] Elango, *Bimbia*, 55.
[43] Edwin Ardener, *Coastal Bantu*, 77.
[44] Roland Oliver, *The African Experience*. (London: Pimlico, 1994), 120

As already noted, many Bakundu slave owners assimilated slaves into their families.[45] The most fortunate were perhaps those who were servants in ruling houses, where many hands made light work, and where loyalty combined with detachment from local kinship ties led to promotion and privilege, like Joseph the son of Jacob, who was sold into slavery in Egypt and is the best known of countless such examples.[46] This state of affairs changed during the years of the trans-Atlantic Slave Trade where African labour was needed in the New World to work in plantations.

The status of a slave might change over time. When first acquired, especially by the rich, a slave's position was one of bondage and he was essentially dehumanised. In theory he had no rights and everything he earned or acquired belonged to the owner. But over time as he learnt the language and customs of the society, he was integrated into the owner's lineage. Furthermore, his children might not inherit his slave status. Thus, freedom and slavery were not binary opposites that they were in the west.[47] There was a continuum in degrees of freedom and servitude. One started as a household slave, then later found one's self neither absolutely free nor absolutely slave,[48] an ambiguous and troubling identity.

The forces of modernity like education in missionary and government schools, as well as other secular values, did much to undermine and eventually destroy slavery. The institution of slavery underwent changes with the coming of Christian missionaries and the introduction of colonial rule. The Christian teaching of equality and the introduction of

---

[45] Conversation with Chief Samuel Ndome at Kake on 26 August, 2007.
[46] Roland Oliver, *African Experience*, 120.
[47] Erik Gilbert and Jonathan T. Reynolds. *Africa in World History* (New York: Prentice Hall, 2004), 124.
[48] Ibid.

western education which provided new opportunities for upward mobility helped to undermine the institution and changed the status of slaves. For example, there is evidence that it was the children of slaves and other groups like outcasts who first enrolled in the newly-created missionary and state schools and were also among the first converts to Christianity.[49] Consequently, they were among the first to be employed as clerks, interpreters, catechists and teachers. Under colonial rule, they won their freedom in principle although they still suffered the stigma of being of slave descent.

There were villages in Bakunduland like Konye and Bole which kept and traded in slaves and during the era of the slave trade Douala, Bimbia and other places on the Cameroon coast became established slave markets and the most important was Rio del Rey. Citing Elango, around 1800 a slave could be bought in the Ambas Bay, Bimbia area, for two handfuls of cowries or three measures of Spanish wine.[50] This was also true of Bakunduland. As Chilver noted, in the Bamenda Grassfield in the nineteenth century, the price of a slave was twenty pieces of cloth.[51] Yet, the extent of slave dealing among Bakundu is not fully known, although as late as 1922 slaves existed in some villages as shown in Table 5.

---

[49] See Nkwi, *Traditional Government*.
[50] Elango, *Bimbia*, 38.
[51] Chilver, "Nineteenth Century Trade in the Bamenda Grassfield" Africa and Ubersee, Band XLV, 239.

Table 5: Bakundu Slave Census by village, 1922

Village	Number of slaves
Bombe	30
Banga	16
Kombone	24
Kombombo	10
Bole	28
Kake	36
Nake	17
Marumba	15
Mabonji	09
Konye	11
Total	**196**

Source: File No. Ae 37/807/22 Assessment Report on Bakundu and Mbonge Tribes, Kumba Division, Cameroon Province. NAB.

From these statistics one may conclude that the institution of slavery was not of great significance among the Bakundu.

Trade routes and markets

Bakundu trade routes were specialised in the traffic of specific commodities.[52] For example, between the fourteenth and fifteenth centuries, the route from Banga to Bakweriland specialised in the sale of ivory, venison and slaves; the waterway from Bombe to Douala specialised in palm produce, baskets and bags, salt, slaves and, with the coming of Europeans around the sixteenth century, goods like tobacco, alcohol, textiles and household utensils; and the western route from Ngongo along River Meme, dealt in palm produce, fish, venison, salt and salves. These were exchanged for trade goods like textiles, tobacco, and especially salt which was not only a food item but also a nutrient for goats.[53]

---

[52] Conversation with Chief Samuel Ndome, Kake, 10 April 2006.
[53] Ibid.

These routes linked many markets which existed where the people exchanged their commodities. Markets in any given Bakundu village were regularly held on specific week days.[54] Wone and Konye markets were the best attended in northern Bakundu as they served members of other ethnic groups like the Balong, Bafo, Ngolo, Mbonge, Bima and Batanga.

Writing about the trade with Bimbia, Elango identified major trade routes connecting Bimbia on the coast with the hinterland. He noted that Bimbia's hinterland potentially stretched to Bamenda grassfields in the north and could be divided into immediate and remote hinterland.[55] Many people in the immediate hinterland are therefore secondary middlemen. The two routes were described as the creek route and the overland route. The more important of these routes which concerns us was the overland route to which the Bakundu were connected. However, indirectly the overland route and its secondary links were important because it traversed the Bakundu-Bakweri-Balong region which was noted for its large herds of elephants.[56] This route was used by the Bakundu to trade with the Bakweri along the coast in things like ivory and palm oil.

In southern Bakundu, Banga, Kwakwa, Bole, Bombe and Ngongo markets attracted buyers and sellers from long distances like Bakweriland, Balong and Mbonge to exchange a variety of goods which included smoked venison, known locally as "bush meat", palm products and European goods like alcoholic beverages, tobacco, mirrors and machetes and other hardware as well as luxuries like textiles, shoes, lamps, etc. Apart from the exchange of commodities, these markets were also places where people socialised, thus promoting and

---

[54] Ibid.
[55] Elango. "Bimbia", 65 – 66.
[56] Ibid. 71.

strengthening inter-ethnic contacts, however indirectly. This promoted further exchange of goods and ideas which broadened the horizons of the Bakundu.

The creek route followed the creeks and mangrove swamps which line the Cameroon coast and was used by canoemen who could thread their way easily through the maze of creeks and swamps in their canoes to reach the districts of Isangele, Balundu and Mbonge in the west, and Mungo Valley and the Cameroons River in the east.[57] The natives sold palm oil, palm kernels and wild rubber to the traders from Bimbia and used the money earned to buy cloth, salt and other luxuries from Bimbia and Duala middlemen.

The Mungo River was a secondary route that provided a link between the Duala and Bakundu.[58] It was on this waterway that European factories were located under German and British rule, perhaps even before. Goods were relatively easily transported along it to the coast for onward transmission to Europe. Messrs. Spear and Co. had a small factory at Bombe under a new man, while Messrs. John Holt and Co. also had a factory at Mundame on the Mungo.[59]

In the western part of Bakunduland, the Meme River provided another tertiary route by which the Bakundu and the Mbonge travelled to the creek area of Rio-del-Rey and onto Calabar in Nigeria.[60] On this route Messrs Woodin and Co. Ltd did business at a small factory managed by a European at Mbonge Marumba. Trading activities were not limited to the Bakundu and their immediate neighbours but extended to parts of eastern Nigeria through Rio-del-Rey.[61] Palm oil seemed to be the main article of trade. According to Comber, the Bakundu traded principally in palm oil of which they

---

[57] Ibid.65 – 66.
[58] Ibid.
[59] Dundas and Carr, Assessment Report. NAB.
[60] Ibid.
[61] Ibid.

produced and traded in large quantities, mostly to Calabar through the network of creeks connecting that river with Rio-del-Rey.[62]

That trade flourished in Bakunduland is clear from these accounts. This was relatively well developed by the fifteenth and sixteenth centuries.[63] The first Bakundu to establish contacts with European traders were the Southern Bakundu. By the nineteenth century, Bakundu in particular, and the Bakundu economy in general fed into the international economy in the era of legitimate trade. The Germans obtained tropical products like rubber and palm products from Bakunduland and sold European products to the local population.

Succession and Inheritance
The Bakundu are patrilineal and the Bakundu society is organised around kinship principle, which determines the right and duties of the individual and his lineage.[64] The oldest son succeeds his father by the rule of primogeniture and at his father's death the son's duty is to preserve his wealth on behalf of his siblings. On the other hand, the oldest son could represent his father in meetings of associations to which the father belonged if he had been initiated into them. In modern times, these traditions of inheritance have evolved. A son or daughter can now inherit the property of any of the grandparents. Such situations arise when parents have only married daughters who by tradition are considered members of their husband's families. The sons of a married daughter can then inherit from their maternal grandparents. On the

---

[62] J. T. Comber, "Explorations from Mount Cameroons and journey through Congo to Makuta". *Proceedings of the Royal Geographical Society* (New Monthly Series) Vol. 1879. 231.
[63] Ibid.
[64] Victor C. Uchendu cited by Vincent B. Khapoya, *The African Experience: An Introduction* (New Jersey: Prentice Hall, 1994), 29.

other hand, such situations may arise when rich grandparents wish to will their property to all their grandchildren: this is more radical, – a clear example of how the Bakundu are adapting to changing times. This was however exceptional for those who felt their relatives could benefit from their toil

Some families that formed a new class were Motuba of Kake I, Bebe of Banga, Mediko of Konye, Njea of Kake Bokoko and Itoe of Bombe. These are among what some historians have called "new men", a semi-traditional and semi-modern and modernising elite. A number of factors made them prominent. As earlier noted, these men were well known throughout Bakunduland and beyond for their relative wealth and their close ties with the colonial authorities. They were some of the first Bakundu families to receive western education which enabled them to exercise political influence or power over their people. With their wealth, people like Bebe of Banga and Mediko of Konye, became ethno-philanthropists of sorts by helping less fortunate Bakundu. This encouraged other Bakundu to emulate them when they became wealthy under German and British rule.

Table 6: Prominent Bakundu families under Colonial Rule.

Name	Village of origin
Ngeti Nambire	Banga
Etukeni Dibuma	Ndoi
Mamweko	Kokaka
Abia	Mbakwa
Mongo	Itoki
Sakwe	Kombone
Diange	Banga
Makumba	Kombombo

Source: File No. 663/76/1923 A. Intelligence Report on the Bakundu Tribe of Kumba Division, Cameroon Province, NAB.

Although wealth, education and close ties with Europeans played a part in creating these new men, it was religion that actually determined the way of life in Bakunduland.

Bakundu religious beliefs regulated aspects of social life, and anything that deviated from them was considered dangerous for social harmony. Bakundu religious beliefs were determined by social and cultural conditions, the physical environment, their past experiences, and their individual and collective needs. They believed in God, of a Supreme deity, who created the universe and everything in it. The Supreme Being was/is assisted by lesser deities each of whom performed a specific function among the Bakundu like the god of rain, that of fertility, of the forest and of evil whom they consulted in times of need. These lesser deities were God's assistants who looked after God's creation.

The Bakundu also believed in spirits which did not have concrete physical form. These spirits were associated with certain physical forms or forces in the sky with objects such as the moon, sun, sky, rain and wind while the earth objects were forests, hills, mountains and metals. There were also spirits of people who died and who were/are relatives in the distant past or more recently. These spirits were invisible. The Bakundu belief in spirits included belief in ancestors, the living dead who were active in society. When a person died, he/she became a spirit with special attributes that made him/her powerful than living beings. As spirits, they acted as intermediaries between God and the living. There were bad and good spirits. The good ones protected the people while the evil ones harmed them.

Politics and Government

One generalisation that can be made about political systems of pre-colonial Africa is that there were two broad types: centralised states and "stateless" societies. In centralised states there were bureaucracies which performed specialised functions such as collecting taxes, supervising ceremonies, entertaining dignitaries, and serving the king or chief. The "stateless" societies, on the other hand, were politically decentralised polities with no bureaucracies. The bureaucrats were chosen from the lineage heads and titleholders. In these decentralized systems, social groups like age-sets, age-grades, "secret societies" played a more prominent role in the maintenance of law and order and helped to harness the resources of the community for collective goals.[65]

    The Bakundu have a "stateless" or decentralised political system. The village is the basic socio-political unit comprising several lineages sub-divided into extended families. Each village was a self-governing community with a village council headed by *moele mboka* or "father of the village" some of whom later evolved into a "chief" or "Headman" under colonial rule. The council was made up of lineage heads, members of secret societies, titleholders, age groups and priestly associations which acted essentially as interest groups. The main function of the village council was

---

[65] Khapoya, *African*, 60.

to settle disputes among the villagers and to ensure internal and external security. In fact, politics and government at the village level were "an exercise in direct democracy"[66] meaning that all views of all groups were heard and the decisions were then declared publicly after being sanctioned by the "holy men" in keeping with the customs and traditions of the people. These holy men were usually title holders whom the people trusted, men believed to be upright and sincere in all that they did in the society. Chiefs and elders were involved in government, and their powers overlapped but were mutually reinforcing. This simply means that these gerontocrats controlled the affairs of the community because they and no one else were believed to understand the needs of the people. They were the ones who consulted the oracles, appeased the gods and performed rites of purification when need arose. Therefore, the welfare of the village rested on their shoulders. However, this system was modified before colonial rule as old men recruited young men into secret societies to ensure continuity.

Some political anthropologists claim that the values that permeate and sustain African societies can be divided into two: first, instrumental values that enable them to readily adjust to new ideas. The Ibo and Kikuyu are the best examples.[67] Their instrumental values enabled them to adopt new ideas and techniques because they yielded desired benefits; second, consummatory values, which people were reluctant to change for fear of offending the ancestors and incurring their wrath. All of these had to do with the people's belief system. They saw their ancestors as a link between the living and the dead. It was believed that societies functioned well because of the role these ancestors played in community's daily affairs. Consummatory values linked new

---

[66] Ibid., 22.
[67] Ibid.

ideas to the ultimate spiritual ends of the community, and were thus hard to discard even if they were deemed to obstruct change. New ideas were therefore assimilated with difficulty.[68]

Faced with the colonial intrusion the Bakundu were able to adapt less painfully than some of their *Orocko* neighbours like the Balue and Mbonge. Politics and government involved all the levels of their society with household, lineage heads, members of secret societies and title-holders playing important roles. At open-air meetings everyone could participate in debates, after which the elders retreated to deliberate and reach decisions. Decisions reached were in keeping with custom and tradition. This process involved a judicial element but was not as peaceful as it sometimes seemed. Dissent was considered before final decisions were reached. This state of affairs existed before European rule was introduced in Bakunduland which led to the appointment of chiefs.

According to John Moki, there were no chiefs among the Bakundu before the introduction of European rule.[69] The title of "Chief" was invented by Europeans before effective colonial rule in the fifteenth century to designate different categories and grades of leaders in various non-western societies. The *Moele Mboka* or "Father of the village" did not deal with Europeans because of his high standing in the Bakundu society. He did not speak to strangers. Talking to strangers was considered by his subjects as an abuse of his authority. He had emissaries to Europeans who were of the lower class in Bakundu society. They had no wealth and the families into which they were born were not influential. Having established contacts with Europeans, such people

---

[68] Ibid., 60.
[69] Interview with John Moki at Kake I, on 10 April 2007. He was among the first Bakundu at Kake to acquire Western education and is a village notable.

became intermediaries between Europeans and the Bakundu society. Some of them were later named chiefs by colonial authorities because they had acquired new skills like reading and writing, and became interpreters, and so acted as middlemen between the villagers and Europeans.[70] The "chief" was sometimes a "headman". Thus, the position of the *Moele Mboka* was transformed into a chieftaincy under colonial rule. The society reacted negatively to such people because of their lowly origins. This was a potential source of tension between the men of influence and the less privileged members who were beginning to gain prominence because of their acceptance of Western values especially western education. Their children received education and eventually won the recognition of the Whiteman, and in so doing formed a new social class.

Moki's claim that the title "chief" originated with Europeans is supported by Tarikhu Farrar[71]. He notes that the word chief came into the English language from old French, in the form of *chef*, during the Norman period, deriving from the Latin *caput* (head). In its usage as a noun during this early period, it simply referred to a leader or head of an organized group of people, that is, a settlement, a civic organization, a military organization, and so on. It denotes leadership of a clan, ethnic group, or a small uncivilized community. Although Tarihku did not write about the Bakundu, what he said applied to them as new leadership style introduced by Europeans was already taking place.[72]

Nevertheless, the institution of *Moele Mboka*, initially hereditary, eventually became elective with the introduction of colonial rule, especially when traditional political

---

[70] Ibid.
[71] For details, see Tarikhu Farrar "When African Kings Became "Chiefs" Some Transformations in European Perceptions of West African Civilization, c. 1450-1800. *Journal of Black Studies*, December 1992, 258-277.
[72] Ibid.

institutions began undergoing change and chiefs were increasingly appointed. Usually, those who governed the village were recognised by Europeans and some naturally preserved this status in their families.

In any case, the choice of a chief was not easy. The person elected chief had to be a man of outstanding qualities and one of these was bravery and wealth. Wealth was measured by the size of the chief's retinues, farms, properties which in Bakundu was known as *boli*. Upon his death, *Moele Mboka* or "chief" was succeeded by any of his sons who was deemed competent and knew the traditions of his people well. If there was no son qualified, any other person from a different family or collateral line was elected to succeed him.

At his enstoolment, the chief was presented with a number of items including a fly wisk, an iron staff, cloth and a wooden stool covered with the skin of a tiger. These insignia were the traditional symbols. The iron staff especially was an emblem of office handed down the generations. As already noted, iron was obtained through trade especially as there are no accounts of iron deposits or industries in Bakunduland. Iron emblems were an innovation inspired by contact with iron smelting peoples. Before that these emblems were made of wood.[73]

---

[73] A.J.H. Latham. *Old Calabar 1600-1891* (Oxford: Oxford University Press, 1978), 25.

An iron staff –One of the symbols of authority

Secret societies or secret associations were important institutions among the Bakundu and played a variety of functions most notably a judicial function. They were called "secret societies" by Europeans who did not know or understand their rites, protocol and codes of communication among members. Only those who qualified to be members were admitted.[74] To become a member, certain conditions had to be fulfilled. Among these were the payment of a fee and lavish entertainment of the members after initiation. Table 7 is a list of the various societies and their admission fees.

The functions of these societies were religious, judicial, commercial and social, and each of these societies had a hierarchy of grades. *Nyankpe* for example was the highest grade of the *Ekpe* society among the Efik of the Calabar[75] region in Nigeria but among the Bakundu, it was

---

[74] Interview with John Moki at Kake I on 10 April 2006.
[75] Latham. *Old Calabar*, 36.

one of the highest secret societies suggesting that it owed its origin from Nigeria. *Nyankpe* operated for the well-being of the community and performed such functions like the enforcement of the law, imposed fines on offenders and the most important was the economic function as it had power to enforce the repayment of debts, an essential power in a society which had adopted credit trading.[76]

Nyankpe was a male secret society which was based on variation of leopards or tigers, animals which were considered very wild among the Bakundu. The use of the skins of these animals was a symbol of authority reserved only for a select few. Any hunter who killed any of these animals was given a title for his bravery. The heads of these animals were preserved and only members of the highest grades of the *nyankpe* society could use them or display them during important village festivities. It is likened to the *Poro* of Sierra Leone and like the *Poro*, it had "inner councils" which were the executive arms of government in the society.[77]

The inner councils made public appearances only at important ceremonies like the death of a titleholder, chief or any of its members, or if the security of the village was deemed to be threatened. They performed rituals of cleansing by invoking the spirits of the ancestors. They usually met in the town hall or *etana*, located in the centre of the village to conduct their business. They made decisions concerning war and peace, about hunting in particular forests, and set the dates for purification rites in villages.[78] Although this system underwent some changes with the coming of European traders and missionaries, and eventually during colonisation,

---

[76] Ibid., 38.
[77] Walter Rodney, *A History of the Upper Guinea Coast, 1545 – 1800* (Oxford: Clarendon Press, 1970), 67 – 68.
[78] Discussion with Chief David Ikoh Besingi at Kumba on 16 April 2006. He is the Chief of Ibemi Bakundu.

secret societies like *nyankpe* endured and still performed their traditional role in a modern context despite strong European hostility and efforts to abolish them. This explains why titleholders are still highly regarded in Bakundu society. It is important to note that the role of *nyankpe* complemented that of government in enforcing laws as the two organs worked closely with each other to ensure peace and security in Bakundu society.

Table 7: Admission fees into Bakundu secret societies

Type of society	Entrance fees
Kolle	Six goats, five pieces of cloth, two bags of salt, six chickens, sixteen legs of venison.
Basongo	Two goats, five chickens, five legs of venison, two bags of salt, one calabash of oil.
Ku	Five goats or one cattle, twelve legs of venison, four chickens, two bags of salt.
Disua	Two goats, twelve legs of venison.
Difoni	Five goats or one cattle, twelve legs of venison, four chickens, two bags of salt.
Ekuka	Five goats or one cattle, twelve legs of venison, four chickens, two bags of salt.
Maloba (Women)	One bag of salt, four legs of venison, a tin of palm oil, twelve heads of tobacco.
Nganya	Two goats, ten legs of venison, three chickens, five pieces of cloth, one bag of salt, one tin of palm oil.
Male	Two goats, ten legs of venison, three chickens, five pieces of cloth, one bag of salt, one tin of palm oil.
Nyankpe	One goat, four legs of venison, one chicken, one head of tobacco.

Type of society	Entrance fees
Bolemba	Four legs of venison, one chicken, one head of tobacco.
Dioh	One goat, one chicken, two heads of tobacco, one tin of palm oil.

Source: File No. Ae 37, Assessment Report on the tribal areas of Mbonge and Bakundu, NAB.

Bakundu religious beliefs were determined by social and political conditions, physical environment in which they lived/live, their past experiences and their collective needs and goals as a people. These beliefs were part of Bakundu spiritual infrastructure. They helped to socialise every Bakundu person and to legitimate ancestral ways, including law and order. All these beliefs helped in the enforcement of law and order in Bakundu society especially as they were conscious of the fact that good fortune could only come if society adhered to their tradition by doing the right things which would not offend God and the spirits of their ancestors.

There is some controversy among scholars about what colonialism did to the power of chiefs. Sometimes, colonialism expanded their authority over larger populations and territories than traditionally enjoyed. The warrant chiefs of Iboland are probably the best example of this process.[79] In Bakunduland the authority of each chief was limited to his village but he consulted other chiefs in matters like the security of his people when need arose. He derived powers from his people including secret societies, and was accountable to them. Before colonial rule, any chief who violated the traditions of his people was severely fined; in extreme cases a chief could be deposed and replaced if he

---

[79] Erik Gilbert and Jonathan T. Reynolds, Africa in World History: From Prehistory to the Present (New Jersey: Prentice Hall, 2004), 293.

was deemed to disrespect tradition. Under colonial rule, chiefs in Bakunduland who did not cooperate with the colonial authorities were deposed. This was the case with the chief of Nake who was deposed by the German colonial officials in 1901. On the other hand, chiefs who cooperated with colonial officials received support because they served colonial aims.

The traditional government sketched above ensured law and order in Bakunduland. The Bakundu norms governed their society and sanctioned their violations. This explains why they were aware of the punishments for crimes like murder or theft. Diviners consulted oracles in the investigation of crimes and where there were doubts, an oath was administered to suspects and the commonest oath seems to have been the sasswood ordeal.[80] If a suspect vomited it, it meant he/she was innocent, but if he/she did not, he/she was killed. Today, oracles no longer exist in Bakunduland because of Western influence especially Christianity.

Closely related to these oracles which were part of Bakundu belief system was the role religion played in the lives of the people. Religion is defined as a set of beliefs and practices related to sacred things that unite adherents into a single moral community.[81] Religion deals with the most basic questions that human beings have been grappling with from time immemorial such as life and death, the deity, and the forces that influence their lives.[82]

For the Bakundu then, everything that happened to them had a religious undertone. Poor or good harvest, low or high birth rate, illnesses, peace within the society as well as their relationship with other people were all linked to their

---

[80] Ngoh, *Cameroon*, 116.
[81] For details, see Vincent B. Khapoya, *The African Experience: An Introduction* (New Jersey: Prentice Hall, 1994), 52. John S. Mbiti, *African Religions and Philosophy*. Second Edition (Oxford: Heinemann Education Publishers, 1990), 1-5.
[82] Ibid.

beliefs in a supernatural being. There was nothing that happened without a cause. Religion therefore helped in shaping Bakundu society.

Individuals in Bakunduland distinguished themselves by their attainments and were awarded titles. The highest honorific title among the Bakundu is *Mutia ku* and *Okia* is the next highest and only one person holds it at any time throughout Bakunduland. Today, it has been modified to read as *Tata Okia wa Bakundu*. This originated in mid 1980s to cement the relationship between the Northern and Southern Bakundu clusters. It meant that the Bakundu are one no matter their region of origin. The criteria for the title are not traditional. The person holding it is chosen because of merit. The person chosen is one who has contributed to development of Bakundu society in many ways.

The title of *Okia wa Bakundu* was evidence that the Bakundu were beginning to evolve towards a trans-village solidarity and integration. The holder of this title was considered sacred in the sense that he was believed to be an embodiment of Bakundu ancestral spirits, and the term for such persons is usually "charismatic". He was believed to possess supernatural powers and to know everything that happens in society by day or night, indeed everything that happens on earth and above. Today, Chief Henry Namata Elangwe of Kake I holds the title of *Okia wa Bakundu*.

Chief Tata Okia Henry Namata Elangwe

Chief Elangwe is in every sense a modern man and a modernizer. Educated at St. Joseph's College, Sasse, from 1947 – 1952, he later studied Pharmacy in Yaba School of Pharmacy, Nigeria from 1952 – 1955. In 1955 he returned home and he was employed by the Cameroons Development Corporation (CDC). After a few years of service with the Corporation, he resigned and began private practice in 1959. He established the first pharmacy, Premier Pharmacy, in Kumba and provided free services to many Bakundu who were unable to pay for their healthcare. In addition, he used some of his wealth to educate young Bakundu and members of his immediate lineage. Among these were people like late Dr. Andrew Kemba Mosongo, Director of Linguistic Centre Buea, Isaac Balemba who was Senior Registrar of the Kumba High Court and also Rose Ituka, a social worker in Kumba acknowledged the support they received from him.

In 1959, he was elected secretary of the Cameroon Peoples' National Congress (CPNC), the opposition party in Southern Cameroon House of Assembly and after reunification of the two Cameroons was appointed Secretary of State for Finance in West Cameroon and Deputy Prime Minister. He was later appointed Minister of Mines and Power in the government of the Federal Republic, a position he held up to 1979. When he left the government, he returned to his native village of Kake I and continued to run his pharmacy.

While in government, he counselled his people on the virtues of working together to promote their development. It is this commitment to the welfare of his people that led to his appointment as Paramount Chief of the Bakundu. Titleholders like him were usually successful men who achieved high status through their personal merit and accomplishments. Elangwe is at home in traditional society and able to understand and withstand the demands of modern society. Little wonder that he was also the president of the Bakundu Cultural and Development Union (BCDU). Recognising his contributions to Cameroon's political progress, the government in 2002 appointed him Chairman of the Cameroon Development Corporation, a position he held till his death in 2014.

Conclusion
This chapter has described the traditional socio-cultural system of the Bakundu to provide the context for subsequent discussion of the direction and depth of change under European colonial rule. It has shown that the Bakundu are a Bautu-speaking people who share a forest environment with their neighbours and kinsmen. Basically peasant agriculturalists, they also lived by hunting, fishing and weaving in pre-colonial times to provide their basic needs. With rudimentary technology of machetes and hoes, they

mastered the difficult forest environment and made use of the opportunities provided by the land endowed with natural resources that have sustained the population.

The Bakundu were not completely self-sufficient though; they depended on the products of other communities too. This encouraged barter trade and, eventually, the creation of trade routes and networks within and beyond their region. Trade between these communities intensified with time paving the way for further socio-cultural contacts. It eventually expanded into trade with Europeans through which the Bakundu acquired European wares while the Europeans obtained tropical products.

Inevitably, culture contact through trade was accompanied by the diffusion of ideas and techniques that led to further changes in the way of life, the customs and beliefs which held Bakundu society together. Even in their dealings with their kinsmen and neighbours, they adopted what they considered useful and rejected what they felt was not. This acceptance and rejection was the crucial innovation which eased the tension and pain in the transition to modernity. This flexibility of the Bakundu indicated their ability to adapt to circumstances. The resulting changes reflected their capacity to adjust which played a part in their acceptance of new ideas such as Christianity, Western education, and new forms of government and politics.

Although segmentary, Bakundu government was representative in nature because representation in village councils comprised all the groups within the society. Even though there were no bureaucracies, the overlapping and mutually reinforcing roles of various groups provided the system with its own mechanisms that enabled it to function smoothly and effectively. Thus, secret societies were executive arms of the government, executing and enforcing laws made by the council. For his part, the chief did not rule alone. He was assisted by a council that was a check on his power. Broadly speaking, the government centred on the direct participation of all villagers. In this regard, one can argue that the basis for political change was already prepared before the coming of Europeans. Thus, the European presence in Bakunduland marked a new beginning in Bakundu relations with the external world. The struggle for change often seemed to be about who benefited from any innovations and whether the society would remain static while its neighbours experienced change in all aspects of human endeavour. These and other issues are pursued in subsequent chapters.

CHAPTER TWO
THE COLONIAL SITUATION

Introduction

Colonial rule in Bakunduland as elsewhere in Africa impacted traditional African life significantly. Politically, Bakundu lost their sovereignty to Europeans. Loss of political sovereignty also meant loss of economic autonomy as well as power to make decisions about law and order, justice and a whole range of issues affecting personal and community life. This meant the suspension, modification or outright abolition of indigenous institutions and practices which the colonial regime considered inconvenient or repugnant. In effect, this was the colonial situation: new unequal power relation between colonizer and colonized. This loss of political power by the Bakundu started with German colonial rule and continued under the British mandate.

The German Period

As early as 1884, the Germans realised that little or nothing could be done in Cameroon without the cooperation of the local people. The Germans proposed that native participation should be considered in the administration of German colonies. Under the leadership of Wilhelm Solf, the last German Colonial Secretary, Germany introduced its own version of indirect rule in Cameroon. This was in the latter part of 1913 when Solf after a tour of inspection to the Cameroons, was readily granted permission to visit Nigeria. As a result of what he saw there, Dr. Solf informed Sir F. Lugard that he intended to introduce the Nigerian system of indirect rule into the Cameroons.[1] With only a rudimentary administrative machinery, the Germans decided to rule using

---

[1] F.J. Moberly, *Military Operations, Togoland And Cameroons, 1914-1916C.* Uckfield, Sussex: The Naval and Military Press, n.d.), 53.ff

indigenous institutions, although, the indigenous institutions especially chieftaincy, had to be modified to suit European needs.[2] As Gann and Duignan point out:

> The Germans, however felt that they could not work through native traditions unalloyed [not mixed with anything else] by efficiency, and they determined greater privilege and larger financial rewards to the chiefs. Chiefs received honorary distinctions, they were allowed to recruit workers for their benefit as a substitute for tribute formerly collected from the subjects, and in exchange for traditional sources of income such as tolls on caravans, they fixed annual stipends of varying amounts. In return for these privileges, chiefs had to supervise tax collection, report diseases, maintain local paths, provide labour to colonial government, afford hospitality to visiting Europeans and perform other such duties.[3]

The significance of this statement cannot be overemphasised. First the Germans modified the functions of chiefs, Bakundu chiefs included, like settlement of disputes and collection of taxes under the colonial regime. Chiefs became the agents of colonial rule and by so doing, gradually lost their power and influence. This arrangement has led Lucy Mair to note that:

> The essence of the new situation that was created by colonial rule was the need of the new overlords for intermediaries between themselves and the mass of the population. Where travelling is slow and difficult and the majority of the population is illiterate, the

---

[2] Harry R. Rubin. *The Germans in Cameroon. 1884-1914: A Case Study in Modern Imperialism* (New Haven: Yale University Press, 1938), 213.
[3] L. H. Gann and Peter Duignan cited in V. B. Amaazee, *Traditional Rulers (Chiefs) in Cameroon History* (Yaounde: Presse Universitaires, 2002), 19.

> execution of government policies must depend upon direct contact to a degree that is hard for westerners to picture. Government needs an administrative staff distributed throughout their territory, who will both make known and enforce the new laws and obligations which they find it necessary to impose. The lowest ranks of his organisation must of necessity belong to the indigenous population. "Indirect Rule" actually means giving administrative responsibility to traditional rulers.[4]

Lucy Mair's statement highlights the role chiefs played in the colonial administration especially in providing law and order. Chiefs acted as intermediaries between the administration and their subjects. Without their involvement, colonial rule would not have been successful. In doing this, the Germans adopted a number of measures. One of these measures was the policy of regrouping scattered settlements into new communities in order to ease collection of taxes as well as reduce government expenditure. In 1906, a law authorised the burning of any isolated hamlet that resisted amalgamation.[5] This law had negative impact on the Bakundu. Many people in villages like Bombe, Banga, Kake and Bole, unwilling to leave their homes, fled to new sites far removed from German control. This destabilised village society in a number of ways. For example, people in the village of Itoki had to begin life afresh at new sites at Mwangale and Mosanja. In their fright and haste, some of them migrated without their shrines and totems.[6] But most importantly, these forced migrations began undermining the traditional authority system since it involved not only

---

[4] Lucy Mair. *New Nations* (Chicago: Chicago University Press, 1963), 100.
[5] File No. Cd/1921/1, Kumba Division Annual Report, 1921, NAB.
[6] Interview with Thomas Ekuka at Mile I, Kumba on 6 November 2007. He is a village notable Kake I and aged 80.

relocation but also some physical restructuring of the village as people began building their houses further away from each other to ensure some degree of privacy.[7]

To ensure compliance with these policies, the Germans also appointed chiefs to replace village heads who were considered too "weak" to govern or too strong to submit to them.[8] Thus, they had to walk a tight rope between pleasing the colonial authority on the one hand and their people on the other. In villages like Nake and Bole, older men were deposed and replaced with younger and more vigorous men.[9] To the Bakundu such appointees were not qualified to rule because many of them were of lowly social origins and status in indigenous society. [10]

The outcome was that appointed "chiefs" at villages like Nake and Bole in Southern Bakundu had the respect of the colonial administration and their families and friends.[11] But they did not have the support of the diehard Bakundu traditionalists who sometimes remained loyal to the deposed chiefs. This created a situation where some villages like Nake and Bole for example had two "chiefs" and divided loyalties. Unrestrained by tradition and backed by colonial authorities, appointed chiefs soon earned a reputation for harsh and

---

[7] Conversation with Peter Ekoi at Kumba on 4 November 2007. He is a retired schools' manager aged 70.
[8] Ibid.
[9] Elsewhere, Charles Atangana was a good example of the newly-created chiefs. He was an interpreter who had served the Germans, in his capacity as keeper of horses (royal stables) in government schools in Hamburg and Berlin. There were other Kamerunians / Africans like him. Later, during the war, he was sub-Lieutenant in the German army. In 1912, in recognition of his services, the Germans named him Chief of Yaounde – Ewondo-people. After the Cameroon campaign, Atangana was interned in Rio Muni with what remained of the German forces. He then asked French permission to return, which was granted. Upon this, the French not only reintegrated him in his old post, but elevated him to the position of Paramount Chief of Nyong and Sanaga region.
[10] Conversation with Daniel Dibo at Tiko on 30 November 2007.
[11] Interview with Chief Samuel Ndome at Kake on 6 November 2007.

rapacious rule. This was a potential source of tension and potential conflict.

The German policy of appointing chiefs caused a lot of resentment in the local population. To effectively retain the respect and loyalty of chiefs, the Germans rewarded them with incentives like owning guns, gunpowder, salt, alcohol, hardware and textiles. These German-appointed chiefs and other Bakundu leaders who were supported by the Germans became representatives of the administration and in most cases these chiefs achieved enhanced status as heads of influential or "prominent families" in Bakunduland.[12]

The enforcement of law among the Bakundu required a system of courts through which the Germans began to introduce innovations in Bakundu customary law. Before colonial rule family disputes were settled by the head of the family, usually the father. At the level of the village, the chief and his council of elders constituted the court. The guilty were fined according to tradition and if they refused to pay incurred a heavier fine to be paid at a specified date. If that period elapsed, they were placed under house arrest known as *moteke*. During *moteke* they could not visit anyone and nobody visited them.

Initially, cases were tried by German officials assisted by interpreters so that native customs could be considered and native languages could be used. This innovation was a first step in the direction of modernization. In 1892 a court of first instance was established at Kombone.[13] The court was administered by a Bakundu notable, Henry Itie, who was the first president of the court. He rendered judgement according to native laws and customs in civil cases where the matter in dispute did not exceed 100 marks. Due to his position, he was

---

[12] For an enlightening discussion of men of prominence see Jan Vansina, *Paths in the Rainforests: Towards a History of Political Tradition in Equatorial Africa* (Madison: The University of Wisconsin Press, 1990) 73-74.
[13] Ngoh, *Cameroon*, 80; Nyenty, "Bakundu Culture", 35.

respected by the people because he was considered fair and incorrupt and incorruptible. He presided over the court for six years and he remained a wealthy farmer. As a result, his family achieved new prominence in Bakundu society.

The second court was composed of a number of chiefs appointed by the German Governor.[14] It kept records of its proceedings and the Governor could attend its sessions or appoint someone to represent him. The court had jurisdiction in matters beyond the competence of the court of first instance. It could impose a maximum jail sentence of two years.[15] The chiefs who presided in these courts wielded a lot of influence and power and were greatly respected in their villages. They formed a class apart in the society. Men like Ngeti Nambire of Banga and Dibuma Etukeni of Ndoi, began to experiment with European and African law. Bakundu jurisprudence began to be harmonised with European legal norms in their rulings. The consequence of this for the Bakundu judicial system was that European jurisprudence began to gradually replace the Bakundu system.

What can be termed the "Dibuma Affair" is a dramatic example of a potential clash between Bakundu and European ideas of justice and a good example of how such clashes could be prevented or resolved. Dibuma was one of the highest Bakundu notables reputed for his occult powers among other things. A young man who had made advances to Dibuma's wife was caught, tried found guilty and hanged. When the matter was reported to the then Governor, Dibuma was summoned, detained and questioned. Before the final judgement, Dibuma was asked what he would like to drink and he asked for brandy, his favourite drink. When he was asked by the Governor why the young man was hanged, he replied that he, the young man, was hanged according to the

---

[14] Ngoh, *Cameroon*, 80.
[15] Ngoh, *Cameroon,* 80; Rudin, *Germans in Cameroon*, 201-202.

law and that had the law not existed, the young man would not have been hanged. The Governor was so impressed with his answer that he released him.[16] This is an example, although a rare one, of the changing European view of the African society from the classic view that Africans were redeemlessly primitive and unprincipled. The Dibuma affair shows the extent to which African norms and values could, with slight modification be used to govern African society. In light of this experience Governor Seitz in 1909 ordered local officials to show "proper" respect for native chiefs and warned administrators against whipping chiefs or weakening their authority.[17] According to a decree of 1913 no chief was to be removed from office and no native was to be appointed chief except with the Governor's approval.[18]

The introduction of taxes, like the appointment of chiefs, caused friction between the Germans and the people. Taxes were a novelty and a tangible reminder that the Bakundu had lost their sovereignty to a new master. They replaced traditional tribute. The result of this innovation was that taxable males began to sell their labour in order to earn money with which to pay taxes. The chiefs were the principal tax collectors and received a five to ten percent rebate on the amount collected. They were also consulted when important policies were under consideration and were given numbered slips of paper to be issued as receipts to those who paid taxes or did tax labour.[19]

British Rule

Under British rule, the Southern Cameroons was first a League of Nations mandate attached to Nigeria and later a U.N. Trust Territory. For administrative purposes, it was

---

[16] Interview with John Moki at Kake I on 10 September 2007.
[17] Rudin, *Germans*, 213.
[18] Ibid.
[19] Ibid.

divided into four divisions, Victoria, Kumba, Mamfe and Bamenda. Lagos was the seat of government but in 1949, Buea became the sub-regional capital of Southern Cameroons with a Resident Governor who reported to the Governor in Nigeria. Each division was administered by a Divisional Officer (D.O.) who reported to the Resident in Buea.[20] In 1922, the Native Authority Ordinance of Nigeria was extended to Southern Cameroons and was the first step toward the introduction of Indirect Rule in the territory. Indirect rule or Lugardism implied the participation of Africans in the management of their affairs. The system built on British colonial experience elsewhere in the empire and is usually attributed to Frederick Lugard, Governor of Nigeria.[21] The British did not attempt to replace indigenous systems of authority some of which had already been modified by the Germans. Rather they ruled through them. The paramountcy of African interests was basic to the system only in theory and when consistent with British interests and norms. Like all imperial powers, the British respected native interests only when they did not clash with theirs. When they did, they (the British) did not hesitate to ride them roughshod. For example, they deposed African rulers whom they did not like. Thus, Lugard noted that indirect rule was:

> … an integral part of the machinery of the administration. There are not two sets of rulers – British and Native working either separately or in cooperation, but a single government in which the native chiefs have well-defined duties and as acknowledged status equally with British officials. Their duties never conflict, and should be complementary to each other and the chief himself must understand that he

---

[20] Ngoh, *Cameroon*, 170.
[21] Gilbert and Reynolds. *Africa*. 290.

has no right to place and power, unless he renders proper service to the state.[22]

Indirect rule offered a number of advantages to the British. First and foremost the system used, where possible, African structures of government. The system required only a small investment in personnel. For example, rather than having British judges in court, existing African judicial systems native courts were used. This did not mean that British authorities were not in charge. The ideology of Indirect Rule assigned the role of overseeing and helping to educate indigenous authorities under British tutelage. As Lugard noted:

> … the primary duty and object of the political officer will be able to educate (the native chiefs) in the duties of the rulers according to a civilised standard, to convince that the oppression of the people is not a sound policy, or to the eventual benefit of the rulers; to bring home to their intelligence as far as may be, the evils attendant on a system which holds the lower classes in a state of slavery or serfdom and so destroys individual responsibility.[23]

A further advantage was that Indirect Rule, with its promise of reforming and modernising local cultural norms and formations in conformity with British norms, was more easily accepted by the people. Thus, the British legitimated their colonial rule with the fiction that theirs was not a mission of cultural conquest, but rather an attempt to "help" the colonised find their own cultural path in the modern world.

In Bakunduland, the British continued the policy earlier practised by the Germans of appointing chiefs where

---

[22] Cited by Amaazee. *Traditional Rulers*, 79.
[23] Gilbert and Reynolds, *Africa*, 291.

there were no chiefs.²⁴ A case in point is that of Chief David Iko Besingi of Ibemi who was appointed chief in 1958 to replace Chief Moto Nebo, who was chief for over thirty years and was deemed too old by the British to govern.²⁵ Under British colonial rule, the Bakundu traditional system began experiencing changes especially with the application of Indirect Rule. Having adopted Indirect Rule as a policy of local administration, the British proceeded to create Native Authorities (N.As.). There were two in Bakunduland, one in Kombone created in 1924 for Southern Bakundu and the other at Ndoi for the Northern Bakundu.

The N.As were a modified institutional framework for Indirect Rule and the mechanism for administering law and order. They had their own bureaucrats and treasuries responsible for collecting taxes. All the revenue from taxes and court fines was paid into the central treasury in Kumba, where the funds were disbursed to the three N.A. jurisdictions. The Kombone Native Court was created in 1924 for the Lower Bakundu villages with Ngeti Nambiri as president, and Ndoi was the seat of the Upper Bakundu court with Etukeni Dibuma as the president.²⁶

Native administration in Southern Cameroon was based on the Nigerian model which recognized and developed native institutions subject to British control to prevent abuses. The constitutional framework of this system rested upon a number of ordinances: the Native Authority Ordinance, the Native Courts Ordinance and the Native Revenue Ordinance.²⁷ Under the 1916 Native Authority

---

²⁴ Elad, "Balkanisation of the Bakundu", 120.
²⁵ However, for the British period, there seem to be no records of the appointment of chiefs for any of the Bakundu villages, perhaps because the British had learnt from the errors committed by the Germans.
²⁶ File No. 105/1921 vol. 1 Reorganisation of Native Administration, Kumba Division. NAB.
²⁷ See Raymond Leslie Buell. *The Native Problem in Africa* (New York: The Macmillan Company, 1928), 688. See also Vincent Khapoya. *The African Experience*, 128-129;

Ordinance, a chief or any other Native was recognized by the government to maintain order and to appoint native police to assist in this purpose. Native courts were controlled by the Native Court Ordinance of 1914 and were composed of native judges who administered customary law. Four grades of courts were recognized under this Ordinance namely Grades A, B, C and D courts which derived their authority from the Resident in Buea. On the other hand, Native Treasuries based on the Native Revenue Ordinance were responsible for levying taxes and collecting revenue and spelt out how these were disbursed.

Under the two colonial regimes, first under the Germans and later the British, the Bakundu lost their political sovereignty. This loss of autonomy however, was partial because the village and kinship basis of politics did not disappear. Councils of elders continued to meet at night or in secret if necessary, and many important matters like marriage transactions, succession and inheritance, even land disputes were resolved without recourse to the colonial state or its agents.

However, this loss of sovereignty affected people's status in society. For example professions like smiths, who were highly respected somehow, began losing their place in society because of European presence as people began adopting European ways. So did titleholders and members of secret societies who traditionally controlled Bakundu society.

There were other effects on Bakundu society caused by the rise of this new class of men. Colonial rule also encouraged disunity among the people which affected their development however indirectly. In 1931, for example, the Bakundu demanded the creation of separate treasuries, a request which was turned down on the grounds "... that it is

---

Erik Gilbert and Jonathan T. Raynolds *Africa in World History: From Prehistory to Present* (New Jersey: Prentice Hall, 2004), 290-294.

not thought possible to remove the native treasury from the close control of the D.O. and none of the ten authorities are yet of sufficient importance or capacity to have separate treasuries".[28] But the real reason for this refusal was the shortage of staff, and the Resident recommended that children be taught Arithmetic in schools to learn how to keep records in order to provide such staff.

The creation of the Kumba Federation of N.A.s in the 1930s to foster development failed because of the mutual suspicion among the ethnic groups of the division. One possible reason for the proposal to create a federation of N.A.s might have been the British desire to break through inter-ethnic differences and foster wider group solidarity for the achievement of the goals of social, economic and political growth. It is difficult to say why this request was made; this was a way of making Bakundu think, act and work as a group although the Bakundu lived in two different clusters that were developing independently of each other. In this way, as a united group, the Bakundu could cope with the competition of their neighbours and kinsmen. Even more important might have been the desire to harness resources in order to foster the development of Bakunduland under colonial rule. A meeting was convened in February 1935 to this end but it was not attended by the Southern Bakundu.

On the occasion of that meeting on 11 February 1935, welcoming the Resident at Ndoi, Chief Mediko of Konye observed that, "... the Bakundu were divided, that they could not agree on proposals for the northern Bakundu. They wanted to preserve clan unity while the southern Bakundu wanted separation". In reply, the Resident of the Southern Cameroons said the Southern Bakundu could not be forced into a single integrated administration, and a unanimous request was made for a court to be re-established in the south,

---

[28] File No. 110/17/1932 Kumba Division Creation of Separate Native Treasuries. NAB.

after the closure of the Kombone court in 1932 because there were no qualified native judges to handle cases.[29] The refusal by Southern Bakundu to join the north in a single court jurisdiction may have been due to their feeling that since they were more Westernised, the northern Bakundu ought to learn from them. This issue was never resolved.

German Economic Policy
The problems facing the Bakundu were not limited to political matters. Under colonial rule, the Bakundu also lost economic power. This was due to the introduction of a modern monetary economy meaning among other things that the barter economy was replaced by a market economy or something close to it. The German and British regimes essentially pursued the same economic policies to serve metropolitan needs. For this purpose they encouraged plantation agriculture, a novelty.

To ensure a steady and abundant supply of tropical commodities like rubber and oil palm produce, Germany promoted plantation agriculture, albeit through private entrepreneurs like Woermann and the Jantzen and Thormaehlen.[30] Ngoh has noted that in order to promote the production of these products, the Germans instituted the Colonial Economic Committee (CEC) whose main responsibility was to study the economic demands of German markets.[31] Its main function was to supply the metropole with tropical products from German colonies. Sub-committees of the CEC were set up to study special problems of agriculture in the colonies to serve European needs.

One of the tropical products in high demand was rubber (*Hevea bresiliensis*), which grew wild in

---

[29] File No. 1524 Letter No. 1338/139 of February 20, 1935. Minutes of a meeting of Bakundu Clan held at Ndoi in January 11, 1935.
[30] Victor Julius Ngoh, *History of Cameroon Since 1800* (Limbe: Presprint, 2002), 54.
[31] Ibid., 81.

Bakunduland. However, the Bakundu did not take easily to collecting wild rubber probably because they did not know its economic value. Nor did they know how to cultivate it. This situation was to change when rubber plantations were created by the Germans at the coast at Lisoka, Kuke, Muscha, Boands, Pobo, Small and Big Puncha, Meanja and Moliwe.[32] Nevertheless, some Southern Bakundu, in villages like Banga, Bombe, Foe, Pete, Nake and Bole, began to collect wild rubber which they sold to Europeans between 1900 and 1913.[33] As the demand for rubber increased, people like Bebe of Banga, Itoe of Bombe and Penda of Pete developed rubber plantations averaging 4 to 5 acres which further enhanced their status and prestige as budding entrepreneurs among their kinsmen.[34]

However, the Bakundu did not have the skills required in rubber cultivation. Among the Bakundu rubber cultivation was not popular probably because they were more attracted to cocoa farming which permitted the cultivation of food staples on the same piece of land. Also, many of them did not have the resources to invest in growing rubber whose financial rewards were unknown to them.

Labour for these plantations was recruited mainly from ethnic groups in the Bamenda grassfields because the coastal peoples alone could not supply enough for a variety of cultural and economic reasons. The labourers were paid monthly wages to enable them buy necessities like clothing, food and medication. Henceforth, plantation and peasant agriculture co-existed and along with them two types of skills in economic production and two kinds of technology. Plantations for the cultivation of cocoa, rubber and oil palm were established along the coast in places like Moliwe,

---

[32] Ibid., 82-83.
[33] Dundas and Carr Assessment Report, NAB.
[34] Ibid.

Ekona, Tiko and Tombel. Although none of the plantations were located in Bakunduland, the new agricultural methods impacted the Bakundu who were encouraged to cultivate these crops. It was the southern Bakundu who first began the cultivation of cocoa because of their proximity to the plantations. Bombe was the first Bakundu village to cultivate cocoa. Itoe Nanyinga from Southern Bakundu was one of the first Bakundu to cultivate cocoa. He was a successful farmer and one of the new monied men. He lived a modest life and encouraged other Bakundu to cultivate cocoa. He owed his success to hard work and his willingness to learn the techniques of cocoa farming. Initially, farm holdings were very small, usually less than one acre and each extended family normally provided its own labour. Their cocoa was sold to Duala middlemen who in turn sold it to European traders along the coast.[35] In the absence of statistics it is difficult to say the amount of cocoa produced and sold and how much was earned in the beginning. The creation of plantations which recruited some Bakundu labour must have been an eye-opener to the greater possibilities or prospects of cocoa farming.

    The Bakundu involvement in cash crop cultivation like cocoa and rubber created labour problems for German plantation owners. This partly accounts for the relative small number of Bakundu plantation labourers. According to Garson's report of 1922, about 40 workers from Upper Bakundu and 55 from Lower Bakundu villages worked in German plantations in Victoria Division for short periods each year for the German period.[36] Table 7 shows the number of Bakundu plantation workers between 1902 and 1906.

---

[35] Conversation with Chief Emmanuel Bebe, Banga, 10 November 2007.
[36] File No. 143/1 vol. Ae G1 Reassessment Report on the Bakundu Tribe Kumba Division, NAB.

Table 7: Plantation Workers from Bakunduland, 1902 – 1906.

Village	Number of workers
Itoki	9
Mbu	8
Ibemi	6
Koba	4
Mbakwa	10
Ndoi	3
Kake	7
Bombe	10
Banga	12
Bole	9
Boa	8
Kombone	9
Marumba	2
Total	**97**

Source: File No. 143 / 1 vol. Ae G1 Reassessment Report on the Bakundu Tribe Kumba Division. NAB.

The number of workers shown in Table 7 cannot be compared with traditional labour mobilisation and use. This created a conflict between wage labour and subsistence labour. The campaigns organised by the Germans in Bakundu villages to recruit labour between 1900 and 1906 caused considerable resentment. To avoid recruitment many Bakundu young men fled to remote inaccessible villages, and those already employed in the plantations left their jobs. The German administration recognised the problem and sought to persuade the people to work for longer periods. German attempts to recruit plantation labourers from inland included the payment of commissions and transport costs to the labourers.[37] One way the Germans retained labour in their plantations was by providing incentives to attract workers among the Bakundu.

In addition, and despite the labour problems noted earlier, the Germans encouraged the indigenous production of cocoa (*Theobroma cacao*) and oil palms by providing the farmers with seedlings and also sending agriculture experts to teach them how to handle and treat cocoa. Today, in addition to cultivating food crops like plantains and cocoyams (*Xantosoma saggitifolium*) the Bakundu are mainly cocoa farmers. The average annual Bakundu production of cocoa was about two to five tons each year, enough earning for more than subsistence.

A cocoa farmer in his farm

British Economic Policy
Interest in cocoa farming continued under British rule. When Britain assumed effective control of Southern Cameroons in 1916, she gave priority to reviving the economy which began to decline at the outbreak of the First World War. The British

---

[37] E. M. Chilver and Ute Roschenthaler (ed). *Cameroon's Tycoon: Max Esser's Expedition and its consequences* (New York, Oxford: Berghahn Books, 2001), 62.

initially focused attention on agriculture and trade. The promotion of the commodity sector which encouraged the production of cash crops like cocoa and palm oil was everywhere welcomed. These economic changes had far-reaching consequences for the people. A monetised economy created new sources of wealth and status. New economic fortunes were bound up with the export of primary products, as the economic system began the shift from subsistence to a modern economy. All these helped to improve the living standards of the people many of whom increasingly engaged in trade.

By the 1920s the demand for cocoa was high and more than half the male population became cocoa farmers. According to A. D. Garson, cocoa cultivation became the main occupation of 75% of the Bakundu and in 1930 production reached 98 tons.[38]

By the late 1920s a bag of cocoa was sold at 12 shillings but dropped to 4 shillings in the 1930s perhaps because of the Great Depression.[39] The average size of cocoa farms varied between one-quarter and five acres, an overall average of two and half acres. This was a novelty. The total number of acres devoted to cocoa farming was estimated at less than 300[40] by 1930, with Itoe of Bombe, Bebe of Banga and Mediko of Konye being the biggest and most prominent Bakundu farmers. However, we do not know how much money they earned, how much acreage they farmed and how much labour they used, because of lack of statistics.

Cocoa and other cash crops brought a social revolution as seen in the emergence of new men of wealth like Bebe, new ways of life, new measures of status, prestige,

---

[38] File No. 143/1 Vol. ARGI AD Garson Esq. Reassessment Report on the Bakundu Tribal Area, 1931. NAB.
[39] File No. 143/1 Vol. Ae GI AD Reassessment Report on the Bakundu Tribal Area, Kumba Division. NAB.
[40] Ibid.

political power and influence in Bakunduland. Despite the Great Depression that led to a fall in the prices, Bakundu continued to produce cocoa in growing quantities as shown in Table 8 because cocoa farming was now deeply ingrained in them.

Table 8: Cocoa Farming in Bakundu Villages in 1930.

Village	Number of bags	Number of farmers
Ndoi	126	23
Konye	75	09
Kokaka	78	20
Wone	72	09
Mbakwa	48	29
Kake	140	30
Kombone	122	21
Marumba	81	20
Nake	84	18
Bole	91	22
Foe	72	16
Total	**989 tons**	**207**

Source: A. A. Garson Esq. ADO Reassessment Report on the Tribal Area of Bakundu, 1930. NAB.

In the absence of statistics for previous and subsequent years, it is difficult to say whether there was an increase or decrease in cocoa production. However, with the growing interest shown in the cultivation of this crop, one can only argue the opposite that producers and production would have been on the increase. By the 1930s, many Southern Bakundu had larger farms, than Northern Bakundu, of about 5 acres on the average which provided jobs for between 5 to 10 workers from other regions of the country, particularly the Grassfields.[41]

---

[41] Conversation with Chief Emmanuel Bebe at Banga on 10 November 2007.

The labour was paid for by a new form of partnership known as the "two-party" system, which is a common practice today in almost all the cocoa growing regions of Cameroon. In this system, the owner of the farm bought the chemicals like gamaline and other inputs such as spear heads and cutlasses for harvesting. The partner, usually a non-native without land, provided the labour. When the cocoa was processed and sold the owner deducted what he had spent for the inputs and the net balance was shared between him and the worker. This was a new form of labour use by the Bakundu and their neighbours and one more way in which they, their neighbours and kinsmen were experimenting as well as transitioning to modern economic forms and ideas. These were developments that emerged with cocoa farming. Eventually, the volume of cocoa produced was undoubtedly the primary reason for the creation of cooperatives.

The Emergence of Cooperative Movements
One effect of the British economic system which made use of the existing Bakundu structures was the development of cooperatives whose impact on the Bakundu cannot be overstated. Inevitably, it contributed to the expansion of cocoa, coffee and rubber farming by providing a ready and modern means of marketing all produce. Villages in the northern and southern Bakundu formed the Cocoa Farmers' Cooperative Scheme headquartered in Kumba. The first cooperative society in Bakunduland was established in 1932 at Kake with a membership of thirty and in 1950 another was established at Konye with fifteen members. In 1952, the third was established at Banga with twenty-eight registered members.[42]

---

[42] File No. Qd/a 1953/3 Intelligence Report on the Bakundu Tribe Kumba Division, Cameroon Province, NAB.

The beginning of the cooperative movement is a clear indication of the growing importance of cash crop farming among the Bakundu. Initially, not many Bakundu showed interest in them but when these Cooperatives began aiding farmers by supplying farm tools like cocoa spraying machines, insecticides and loans to farmers, interest in them grew.[43] Bakundu farmers like Njea of Kake Bokoko, Bebe of Banga, Esoe of Boa and Elangwe of Kake I, all in Southern Bakundu and Mediko and Samuel Motuba of Konye and Etoto of Supe in Northern Bakundu were predictably among the first members. To encourage modern and high yields production, Superintendents of Agriculture were appointed by the government to supervise the proper use of modern techniques like use of spraying machines and application of chemicals to protect the crops against diseases and modern technologies, all in an effort to promote high production and a better quality of cocoa which would eventually benefit the Bakundu and other indigenous farmers financially and economically.

---

[43] Atinda, "Bakundu", 70

First farmer's cooperative society at Konye

Although there are no records to measure the changes then taking place, the involvement by the Southern Bakundu farmers shows the progress of westernisation and modernisation which began in the south and was gradually extended to the north. Inevitably then, the southern cluster became more modernised than the north, because the new ideas were first introduced there. However, the situation changed as the Southerners became complacent while the Northerners, though disadvantaged by their geographical remoteness, worked harder to close the gap between them and their Southern kinsmen. This development can be judged in generational terms because the younger generations in the North took the disparity of incomes between them and the Southerners as a challenge and worked harder to increase their incomes. This trend started in the mid-1950s when many Bakundu who had worked in plantations returned home and started cultivating the land using modern methods of cultivation. In this way, a dynamic of emulation in modernisation and development became an indigenous initiative.

Traditional method of drying cocoa

Furthermore, in October 1927 the British colonial administration introduced N.A. Cocoa Fermenting Scheme at Kumba, Mambanda, Mukonje, Kurume, Ikiliwindi, Nyasoso, Ngusi, Baduma and Kombone.[44] One result of all these initiatives was the construction of ovens to properly dry harvested cocoa especially in the rainy season. Before the introduction of ovens, the Bakundu used to dry their cocoa on barns. They built a barn under which fire was made. This method produced low quality cocoa. The modern method of using ovens provided a more effective way of drying cocoa. Ovens were built with cement and a hole provided through which fire was made inside. The surface of the oven provided enough heat that dried the cocoa. So cocoa dried in such ovens had no direct contact with the smoke like the traditional method. Bakundu villages like Kokaka, Ndoi and Konye were served from the Kurume scheme. The first ovens in Bakunduland were constructed in the 1930s and early 1940s. They were constructed by groups of individuals, sometimes by members of the same kinship group at the cost of about 30 pounds sterling.[45] This had a number of benefits for the individual farmer and eventually the community. It improved the quality of cocoa and the incomes, encouraged the planting of more cocoa, improved and financial social status and prestige, and in the long run, enhanced not only economic prosperity but also political power of individual farmers. This in turn encouraged new efforts in solidarity such as purchasing ovens in all Bakundu villages except Itoki and Mbu where cocoa cultivation still lagged due to the hilly nature of the land.

---

[44] File No. Cd/1928/1/KDAR; 1927. Annual Report for Kumba Division, NAB.
[45] Conversation with John Moki at Kake on 20 November 2007.

The purchase of ovens by groups of individuals is only one example of kinship and ethnic solidarity and of traditional institutions and values adapting to and serving modern economic needs. All farmers who dried their cocoa paid for the service with a specified quantity of cocoa. At the end of each cocoa season, the amount of cocoa collected was marketed and the proceeds distributed to members who used the ovens. Some of the profits were used to maintain the ovens.[46]

An oven - A modern method of drying coca

In the late 1940s and early 1950s some Bakundu individuals began building personal ovens. This was a measure of the rapid economic change which resulted from growing capital accumulation and improved standards of living. Chief Emmanuel Bebe,[47] remembers that his father made about nine hundred pounds or about seven hundred and fifty thousand francs profit a year which he used to expand his cocoa farms, using the proceeds for the education of his children, and to help the less fortunate Bakundu. Thus the idea of capital accumulation and through investment was becoming ingrained, however slowly in Bakundu social values. Table 9 shows those Bakundu who built personal cocoa ovens.

---

[46] Conversation with Abraham Lokiri at Kake I, 10 November 2007.
[47] Conversation with Emmanuel Bebe, Banga 10 November 2007.

Table 9: Bakundu oven census, 1940s and 1950s.

Name	Village (South)	Name	Village (North)
Bebe	Banga	Modika	Koba
Itoe	Bombe	Etoto	Supe
Motuba	Kake	Mediko	Konye
Esoe	Boa	Ituka	Wone
Motanga	Foe		
Mukete	Bopo		
Ndome	Kake		

Source: Conversation with John Moki at Kake I on 14 November 2007.

The number of Bakundu who owned ovens is indicative of the growing importance of cocoa farming or improved living standards and greater involvement in a monetised economy. Despite this expansion food production did not diminish as the people continued to grow cash crops alongside food crops in a system that can be described as mixed farming / agriculture.

Petty Trade and Export Trade

Trade was also an important economic activity in Bakunduland. Palm products, ivory, rubber, and cash crops like cocoa and coffee were major products sold to Europeans by the Bakundu. Gunpowder, trinkets, pipes, umbrellas, mirrors, textiles and liquor were the luxuries imported from Europe. The African Fruit Company (A.F.C) based in Bombe bought cocoa and palm kernels. So did the Deutsch West *Afrikanishe Handelsgesellschaft* at Mbonge.[48] Wealth from the sale of cash crops and other tropical products enabled the Bakundu to buy European luxuries and helped eventually to integrate them into the modern economy. One major consequence was their gradual neglect and eventual

---

[48] File No. Ae. 37/807/22 Assessment Report in Tribal Areas of Mbonge and Bakundu, 1922. NAB.

abandonment of many indigenous arts and crafts, a phenomenon that has been observed elsewhere in Africa and is considered one of the root causes of underdevelopment.[49] Table 10 shows the volume of Bakundu export trade with Germans between 1913 and 1914.

Table 10: German Trade Statistics in Bakunduland in 1913 – 1914.

Product	Quantity (tons)
Palm kernels	366
Palm oil	11
Rubber	3
Ebony	2,460
Cocoa.	2,129

Source: File No. Ae II Intelligence Supplementary Report on the Bakundu Area, Kumba Division. NAB.

The change from barter trade to the use of currency facilitated trade. The German Mark was the legal tender which facilitated exchange. As a result of this change, Bombe, Banga, Ngongo, Kake, Boa, Kombone, Wone and Konye, became important market centres and people from other areas came there to sell their goods and purchase their needs. The presence of two natural outlets, the River Mungo to the east and Meme to the west facilitated increasing trade during German rule. Due to the fact that the rivers provided cheaper transportation, the Germans set up factories at Bombe and Mbonge respectively to evacuate export commodities as already noted.

In regions where regular markets were less common, people nevertheless met to exchange goods profitably. In this process a multitude of buyers and sellers bargained until they

---

[49] E.A. Akintoye, *Emergent African States: Topics in Twentieth Century African History* (London: Longman Group, 1926), 92-93.

arrived at a mutually-agreed price, influenced by the pull and push of supply and demand for a particular commodity. Bakundu markets were controlled directly or indirectly by local authorities, that is, members of the ruling house with the sole aim of making profits. It can thus be argued that by controlling the markets, the chief shared in their day-to-day management as was done elsewhere.

In general a similar system of control existed among the Bakundu. At Bombe, for example, the chief sought to control trade, assisted by members of the secret societies. It was taboo for a commoner to sell ivory or a slave. These were highly priced luxury commodities which only titleholders could sell. To this extent, then, accumulation and distribution of wealth became associated with membership of secret or regulatory societies in Bakunduland. To maintain trade monopoly, the chiefs and members of secret societies engaged in gift-exchanges with their peers and in this way reinforced their solidarity and strengthened resistance against potential competitors who were non-members.[50]

For example, Basil Davidson notes that in Iboland:
> The men of *Arochukwu*, a ridge of country running south eastward from the central Ibo uplands, had become famous for their services of a revered Ibo rock, the *Ebinokpapi*. This was their chief specialisation. They used it as a means of founding and cementing an itinerant trading corporation whose colonies were established, during the seventeenth century, in almost every part of Iboland. ...Through these corporate Aro colonies there was channelled the growing trade of Iboland. House-to-house buying and selling gave way to regular marketing at two great four-day fairs, opened

---
[50] Chilver, Nineteenth Century Trade", 242.

> by Arochuku men at twenty-four day intervals, that were attended by thousands of traders from all over the surrounding countryside.[51]

According to this account, the Ibo were quick to realise the profits they could make from trade if they all joined to protect it, and in this way create a monopoly in Iboland.

This was "regulation" without a modern bureaucracy and it does not seem to have been less efficient than its modern equivalents. Such controls were extended to itinerant traders, who were not allowed to sell goods without the consent of the chiefs and members of secret societies. As Chief David Besingi noted:

> Our society was not an open society where anyone could do what he wanted. Even the coming of Europeans did not change things a lot. Our people carried on trade with the Europeans which encouraged many Bakundu young men to become traders. As far as trade was concerned no non-Bakundu was allowed to trade in any of the Bakundu villages without the consent of our elders. They sold their wares only when they satisfied the demands of our elders. When a trader refused to pay, he was driven away and word sent to the next village not to allow him sell his wares. To avoid this, traders always complied with the demands of our people.[52]

This is evidence that the Bakundu wanted to monopolise trade in their land. The restrictions imposed on trade by the titleholders made it difficult for newcomers to compete. This partly explains why membership of associations like *dio*,

---

[51] Basil Davidson. *The African Genius: An Introduction to African and Culture History* (Boston: Little, Brown and Company, 1969), 99.
[52] Conversation with Chief David Iko Besingi at Kumba on 20 December 2006.

butame and *nyanpke* became a common ambition in Bakunduland even among some so-called educated elites. To maintain the stability and sustain prosperity of the sector, these societies were also debt-collectors for their members and price-control agents for particular commodities like slaves and ivory. Prices of such lucrative items were determined by these associations in order to keep them permanently high and protect the trade monopoly.[53]

The British Phase
German economic activities and operations in Cameroon ended abruptly at the outbreak of the First World War. Nevertheless, the new economic system introduced by the Germans in 1884, although it lasted only 20 years, continued under British rule beginning in 1922. Prices of livestock and food commodities, for example, ranged from one penny to thirty shillings in 1922[54] as shown in Table 11.

Table 11: Foodstuff and livestock prices under British rule

Food stuffs / Livestock	Price
Plantains	1 – 7d a bunch
Cocoyams	3s per cwt.
Egusi	1d a cigarette tin
Goat	8s – 20s according to size
Sheep	8s – 20s according to size
Pig	10s – 30s according to size

Source: File No. 143/1 Vol ARGI A.D. Garson Esq. ADO Reassessment Report on the Tribal Area of Bakundu, 1931. NAB.

All these economic activities, including livestock production for domestic ritual needs created and sustained trade links with other ethnic groups. Although statistics on

---

[53] Chilver, "Nineteenth Century Trade".
[54] File No 143/1 Vol. ARGI AD Garson Esq. ADO Reassessment Report on the Tribal Area of Bakundu, 1931 N.A.B.

the volume of trade in Bakunduland are lacking, it can be argued that under British administration there was an improvement in trade which attracted people from northern areas like the Banyang of present-day Manyu Division, Hausas from northern Cameroon and Nigerians. Some of these people settled eventually in Bakunduland. By 1930, there were 52 resident traders from Banyang country and many Hausa traders and later intensified with the influx of the Igbo from Nigeria.[55] Their presence in Bakunduland impacted their local economy. The Ibo especially dominated petty trade in the Southern Cameroons, a dominance with which Southern Cameroonians could compete only with great difficulty. These processes were irreversible and led to Bakundu involvement in a variety of tertiary economic activities outside the traditional economy. They also occupied prominent positions in the colonial administration and as Chiabi has shown, this helped to fuel anti-Ibo xenophobia and Southern Cameroons nationalism ultimately.[56]

Social Affairs
Although statistics are hard to come by, it seems reasonable to infer that the Bakundu were gradually becoming part of the cash economy. The implications of these developments are difficult to overstate. If the Bakundu were not yet completely Westernised they were now less traditional in their outlook and lifestyle. One way to measure this growing monetisation and is its social impact was especially the number of modern homes built by men like Bebe and Mediko often referred to as *mota' kori*, meaning rich or big man. These modest structures still dot Bakundu villages. They

---

[55] Ibid.
[56] E. Mucho Chiabi, "The Nigerian – Cameroonian Connection", in *Journal of African Studies*; Vol. 13 Number 2, Summer 1986, 59.

reflected the new lifestyle, testifying in their own way to the impact of colonialism as an education in the broadest sense of the term.

First modern house in Bakundland - Bebe's residence

Table 12: Modern houses in Bakunduland in the 1930s and 1960s.

Name	Village	Type of house	Year constructed
Bebe	Banga	Permanent	1934
Itoe	Kake II	Permanent	1950
Itie	Marumba Botondoa	Semi-permanent	1951
Etoto	Supe	Semi-permanent	1951
Misodi	Bole	Semi-permanent	1951
Etoma	Kombone	Permanent	1953
Motuba	Kake I	Permanent	1958
Diony	Kwakwa	Permanent	1959
Bakata	Marumba Boa	Semi-permanent	1960
Ituka	Wone	Permanent	1960
Eboa	Ibemi	Semi-permanent	1960
Mediko	Konye	Permanent	1960
Modika	Koba	Semi-permanent	1960

Source: Martin Atinda "The Bakundu under Colonial Rule, 1897-1961".

The construction of these houses had one significant result in Bakunduland which directly or indirectly affected the Bakundu worldview and identity. Traditionally, anyone who built a semi-permanent or permanent home was said to belong to a cult which "mystically" provided him with wealth. They allegedly paid for this wealth with "human heads". This was and is not unusual as anyone familiar with the Arochukwa cult among the Igbo of Nigeria knows.[57] A parallel in Bakunduland is what was referred to as *ekumutu* or *nyongo*, a cult that is believed to supply wealth to members after human sacrifices were made. Some members were believed to have association with even Bakossi cult which was said to have had its seat at Kupe Mountain. On the other hand, such wealth was also said to come from *ndongole* which is located in the deep waters of Ndian Division. Here, members received bundles in which their gifts were concealed. From these bundles the beneficiaries received things like bumper harvest and many births in their areas of origin depending on which bundle one picked. Some of these bundles contained very bad and dangerous contents like locusts and epidemic like measles. To avoid this association and stigma of being considered a "wizard" people feared building such houses and, in general, flaunting their wealth in other tangible ways. This myth was gradually discarded as many more Bakundu came to associate wealth with one's hard work and frugality. This modified Bakundu traditional beliefs, sometimes radically, and made them realise the benefits of modern ways of raising capital, including belonging to cooperatives and investing in ovens, use of fertilizers and other technologies helped to improve the quality and price of one's cocoa.

---

[57] Basil Davidson. *The African Genius: An Introduction to African and Culture History*. (Boston: Little, Brown and Company, 1969), 99-101.

Conclusion

In the light of this discussion, we can better understand the ambiguous attitude of the Bakundu to colonialism.[58] The colonial administration modified the indigenous structures in which the traditional elite enjoyed a privileged position in society and held all the levers of power in their hands. This shift of power to Europeans showed the new, unequal power relations between the European administrators and the Bakundu traditional elites. But the shift of power was not only to the colonial authorities.

Among Africans, it also shifted from the traditional elites to the small but growing new class of new men like Moses Ebollo and Manfred Okanda who were clerks, and civil servants like Chief Rudolf Duala Itoe and John Nakomo who had mastered some of the new skills introduced by Europeans and had consequently become semi-westernised. Among these skills were reading, writing and counting, in short, Western education.

Such people were considered "bakara" on the one hand. But on the other deviants or worse, wizards, and their behaviour anti-social. Their success was frequently attributed to exotic causes, usually witchcraft and various forms of the occult. Those who built modern houses were believed to be members of very powerful cults, which taught them mystical ways to make money. Ironically, to hold the society together, witchcraft was employed as a mechanism of social control by the members of secret societies. The fear of witchcraft may partly explain why cases of conflict between the traditional elites and the new elites were not reported when new administrative structures were introduced.

Studies appearing before the 1960s centred on the activities of Europeans in Africa but failed to emphasise

---

[58] Margaret Peil, *Consensus and Conflicts in African Societies: An Introduction to Sociology* (England: Longman, 1982), 359.

sufficiently the part Africans themselves played in this process.[59] Contacts between Africans and Europeans intensified in the colonial context and started that complex process of change referred to as "modernisation". Africans were not wholly victims of imperialism. They were acted upon but also influenced the nature of the impact of forces generated by the presence of Europeans. The Bakundu were no exception to this experience. Messengers, clerks, interpreters, traders and farmers who played intermediary roles, individually and collectively, exercised considerable influence in defining the colonial situation and its new dynamic which sometimes produced conflicting roles and tensions in the society. One such area was in the direction, development, expansion and control of trade in Bakunduland.

The European presence, while it was a threat to the traditional elite at first glance, also brought new opportunities. Every Bakundu wanted to enjoy equally the opportunities created by the European presence.

The main European goods were textiles, alcohol, gunpowder, salt and tobacco, while ivory, slaves and palm produce were the chief products sold to Europeans from Bakunduland. Trade alliances and networks were created with traders in Douala in the east and those in Rio-del-Rey and as far as Calabar in Nigeria. These alliances provided security, not only for the traders and trade routes, but also for their goods as they travelled to distant markets.[60] They also helped them to collect debts where necessary. This guarantee of security encouraged long distance trade which was dominated by trade in ivory, slaves and palm produce.[61]

---

[59] Akintoye, *African States*, 2.
[60] Chilver "Nineteenth Century Trade". 240-242
[61] Ibid.

While some Bakundu remained in the villages and produced these tropical commodities to sell, others sold their labour to earn a living. Such wages were used to purchase the things they needed for their upkeep. The more important thing was the acquisition of western education that made them to become more conscious not only about their environment, but how to live a decent life, feed well and cater for the needs of one's family.

The new economic system introduced by the Europeans was welcomed by the people. The commodities sector produced palm oil, cocoa, coffee and rubber for the metropoles. These changes had far-reaching implications for the Bakundu. Directly and indirectly, this economic system ultimately helped to improve the standard of living of the people in general and together with Western education and modern healthcare created a nascent modernising Bakundu elite.

CHAPTER THREE
CHRISTIANITY IN BAKUNDULAND

Introduction
Bakundu society like other African societies is intensely religious.[62] Religion is and was a fundamental factor to their worldview and it exerted the strongest influence on the people's daily life. This fact has been made clear by missionaries and anthropologists who observed that the lives of Africans were largely influenced by religious ideas and institutions. In general, African belief systems and practices varied from one people to the other. Despite these variations, the traditional religions were born of and sustained a strong community life and communal values which required individual participation in ceremonies, rituals and festivals.

The idea of a supreme deity was not new to the Bakundu. They believed in a supreme deity, *Obase,* who could be reached through the spirits of the ancestors and through sacred objects. The forms of this religion may appear simple, even grotesque to the undiscerning observer. These systems of thought and ideas predisposed the Bakundu to missionary evangelisation and was the basis of Bakundu Christianity.

Missionary Explorations, 1873 – 1875
The pioneer phase of missionary efforts at evangelisation in Bakundland began with missionary explorations in 1873 that took missionaries to villages inland like Itoki, Mbu, Ibemi, Supe and Konye. These explorations were intended to open up the interior to missionary effort and to ensure the planting of Christianity there. In most cases, these early efforts met with a lot of resistance from the people who saw this as a

---

[62] John S. Mbiti, *African Religions and Philosophy*, Second Edition (New Hampshire: Heinemann Educational Publishers, 1997), 1.

threat to their traditions. This was followed by the building of churches or the expansion and consolidation phase. The first mission station was opened at Bombe in Southern Bakundu. From here missionaries began their efforts not only to evangelise the people but also to introduce Western values, mainly through schooling. It is against this background that the contribution of missionaries to the gradual transformation of Bakunduland is examined.

The first missionary to reach the interior and contact the Bakundu from the coastal base at Bimbia was Quintin Thomson, a member of the London Missionary Society, in 1873. The arrival of George Grenfell and Thomas Comber in 1875 and 1876 respectively began effective missionary work in Bakunduland. These young men continued the exploration of the interior of the territory. Comber penetrated Bakundu territory to Bombe on the Mungo banks where Thomas Lewis subsequently settled and began effective mission work in 1897 with the building of the first chapel.[63] That same year Bombe had its first resident missionary, the Rev. Nathaniel Lauffer, a Basel Mission Missionary, and in a short time six out-stations were opened in neighbouring Bakundu and Balong villages like Banga, Foe, Pete, Malende, Mundame, Yoke and Muyuka.[64]

Opening of Bombe Station

As the pioneer station, Bombe became a 'model' station of effective commencement of missionary work. The station was built away from the native village. It was located on a hill, in sharp contrast with the village community. The missionary quarter thus provided a striking example of the

---

[63] J. Du Plessis, *The Evangelisation of Pagan Africa, A History of Christian Missions to the Pagan Tribes of Central Africa* (Cape Town and Johannesburg: C Juta and Co., Ltd, 1929), 165.
[64] W. Keller, J. Schnellbach and R. Brutsch, *The History of the Presbyterian Church in West Cameroon* (Victoria: Presbook Printing Press, 1969), 10.

European way of life to which the Africans, consciously or unconsciously would aspire.

Bombe was a complex which comprised the missionary residences, a school, the catechist's house, a dispensary, a chapel and a garden. All of these provided the basis of a "modern" community. The people learned new things from the Europeans which altered their way of life. Initially, there was resistance because African beliefs and ancestor veneration were condemned by the missionaries. This hostility to the missionary presence and effort was common throughout Bakunduland.[65] For example, only a few years after Bombe was built in 1898, the people burnt the church house and had the Christians severely beaten,[66] because the Christians began to question the sacred character of the chieftaincy and its spiritual and secular authority. The Christians now began to see chiefs as only a secular leader whose authority could be challenged.

Traditional Healers
Before the coming of the missionaries there were traditional medicine-men who provided healthcare to the people. The men and women who treated the sick were sometimes called "herbalists" or "traditional doctors" by the Europeans, but were commonly referred to among the Bakundu as *moboa boa* or *nganga*. They were trained by the very elderly people who had been involved in administering treatment to the people for years while some were inspired to become healers through dreams and were told what herbs to use for specific illnesses. Prominent among these herbalists in the 1900s were Ekuka Motanga from Ibemi, Ngoe from Mbu, Sese Mekoli from Pete and Abunaka from Mabonji. There were

---

[65] Keller, Schnellback and Brutsch, *Presbyterian Church*, 49.
[66] Interview with Rev. Elangwe Namaya, Buea, 10 January 2006. He is a Presbyterian Pastor at the Buea Town Congregation.

also female healers like Iya Imbia Sakwe from Kake I and Ongie Motuba from Banga.[67] These healers were highly respected in Bakundu society.

The health of the people was also one of the earliest preoccupations of the missionaries. Basic rules of hygiene and sanitation were taught to the converts and school children and routine checks were carried out to ensure a clean environment. Also, the danger of living with animals in homes was made known to the people.[68] A dispensary was set up at Bombe in 1900 and at Itoki in 1923 where the local population and the members of missionaries' families were treated for malaria, small pox and fever.[69]

According to Mbiti, these medicine-men and women are the most valuable source of help. But they have suffered most from European and American writers who pejoratively call them "witch-doctors".[70] The herbalists and diviners were accessible to everyone and at all times. They used plants, herbs, bones, seeds, roots, potions and sometimes sacrifices of chickens or goats to appease the spirits who were believed to have caused the disease. These healers formed the medical establishment of Bakunduland. They often knew each other and each other's specialty and referred patients accordingly.[71] Ultimately, they formed a "medical network" which shared information about patients and had a good health profile of individuals and the society at large. Treatment of disease and misfortune among the Bakundu was a mixture of religious divination and clinical methods.[72] These medicine-men and women treated sexual impotence and infertility, among other things and were deemed as

---

[67] Conversation with John Moki, Kake I, 15March 2008.
[68] Ibid.
[69] Ibid., 101 – 102.
[70] Mbiti, *African Religion*, 162.
[71] Conversation with John Moki, Kake I, 7 March 2008.
[72] Mbiti, *African Religion*, 165.

"legitimate", because their competence inspired hopes of good health, protection and security from evil forces.[73]

The introduction of Western medicine did not end the traditional methods of healing. Under colonialism, traditional medicine was outlawed and driven, so to speak, underground. Bakundu traditional healers (*nganga*) did not take this kindly and they resisted European attempts to destroy their profession. In 1905, healers like Sese Mekoli of Pete mobilised his colleagues against the Germans and later the British by telling people that Whiteman's medicine was poisonous.[74] In other parts of Bakunduland like Mbu and Itoki, these healers also resisted the missionaries and in some cases open confrontations broke out between the missionaries and supporters of the healers and many converts had to flee for their lives as was the case at Kake in 1890.[75]

One reason for this conflict was economic. The missionaries were a threat to the healers' source of income. However, some missionaries counselled moderation among the converts and asked them to educate their people to accept the new European therapies.[76] Eventually, the Bakundu turned to both Western and traditional medicine, although many of them tended to believe more in the efficacy of the traditional healers.

Despite this state of affairs, the missionaries continued to persuade people to depend more on European medicine provided by the health centre because of its modern methods and therapies.

Missionary humanitarianism, the work of missionaries to promote the material and social well-being of Africans, is often contrasted with their purely evangelistic or

---

[73] Ibid., 166.
[74] Conversation with John Moki at Kake I on 7 March 2008.
[75] Ibid.
[76] Ibid.

spiritual activities[77]. But this is a mistake, for in the final analysis both objectives complemented each other and had the same goal, namely the transformation of African life and society. This missionary humanitarianism characterised the consolidation phase of the missionary effort among the Bakundu which lasted from 1876 to 1897.

Agriculture
Experimentation and innovation in agriculture were an important aspect of the ideology of the "Bible and the plough" which the nineteenth century secular humanitarians had adopted for the "moral" and material "regeneration" of Africa and which was tried with some success in Nigeria under the leadership of Bishop Ajayi Crowther, the first Anglican Bishop on the Niger.[78]

Agriculture was recommended to Africans as a means of producing the articles of legitimate trade.[79] In spite of this slogan, it was not so much agriculture that the missionaries considered the civilising occupation, as the commerce resulting from it.

These new agricultural methods like the use of chemicals were first introduced in the Christian community. One reason for missionary involvement in agriculture was the desire to grow more food to feed the pupils in the boarding schools. In 1890, a garden, was opened at Bombe where new crops like bananas and cassava were grown alongside fruit trees like paw-paw, oranges, lemon and a variety of vegetables like cabbage.[80] In this garden, people were taught new agricultural techniques like the application of compost

---

[77] J.F. Ade Ajayi, *Christian Missions in Nigeria 1841-1891 The Making of a New Elite* (Evanston: Northwestern University Press, 1969), 17.
[78] Ibid.
[79] Ibid.
[80] Martin Atinda "The Bakundu Under Colonial Rule, 1897 – 1961" (M.A. Thesis, University of Yaounde 1, 2006), 44.

manure and mixed farming. The first people to work on this garden were the converts and volunteers, and later wage labourers who experimented with seedlings of lemon and oranges. In this way, the converts and the villagers were able to grow more food and increasingly achieved food self-sufficiency. For the Bakundu, these new experiments in food crop cultivation supplemented the traditional livelihood based on hunting and gathering. The new farming techniques used to cultivate these crops encouraged many people to become involved in agriculture.

In this way, the traditional economy became more diversified as more people adopted new agricultural techniques and crops. Strictly speaking, these were not religious activities. Rather, they were secular activities and usually characterised as humanitarianism, and was part of the effort to improve the material circumstances of the Bakundu. The missionaries realised that they could better succeed in their evangelising efforts only if the living standards of the people improved simultaneously.

Although statistics are lacking to show how much was achieved at this station, it seems likely that these new initiatives began a modest change in the Bakundu standard of living and general economic well-being.[81] In 1920 and 1921, two other stations, one at Kake in the south and the other at Itoki in the north, were established based on the Bombe model. These two stations were not as successful as Bombe, because it took longer to realise the potential benefits by the population of Kake and Itoki since the people were ignorant of these new ideas. The people in the north especially did not welcome these new ideas because they had not been exposed to them like their southern kinsmen who were nearer to the coast. The outcome was the closure of these stations

---

[81] Interview with Peter Ekoi, Kumba, 20 February 2008.

temporarily,[82] but a few years later they were revived and missionary schools created.

Missionary Schooling

Education was a means to an end as well as an end in itself. As a means to an end it facilitated evangelisation, making it possible here as elsewhere in Africa, for converts to read the scriptures. As an end in itself, it was new skills like reading and writing which opened the way to new employment opportunities in church and in government. Bombe was a Christian community and a model of how such a community supposedly worked.

The community comprised the following: a school, dispensary, garden, the missionary's and catechist residence and a chapel. It was a magnet to attract the indigenous people to the new religion and way of life.[83] As with agriculture, Bombe provided such a model in Bakunduland. It was here that Western education was first introduced by the London Missionary Society and from there it later spread to other Bakundu villages and later to the other parts of Southern Cameroons.

Under German colonial rule, western education expanded in Bakunduland. The Germans established the Lehrer Seminary in Buea for educating Cameroonians under British rule. This institution was transferred to Kake and became Teacher Training College (T.T.C.) Kake. Later, it was moved to Kumba as Government Teacher Training College (G.T.T.C.) for training teachers. The Colonial government and missions each established schools but village schools were established by missions.[84] The London

---

[82] Ibid.
[83] LeVine, *Cameroons, From Mandate to Independence*, 70.
[84] Madiba Essiben "Evangelisation et colonisation en Afrique, l'heritage scolaire du Cameroun, 1885 – 1956 cited by Martin Atinda "The Bakundu under Colonial Rule, 1897 – 1961". (M.A. Thesis, University of Yaounde, 1, 2006), 55.

Missionary Society was the pioneer in the spread of western education.[85] Atinda, citing Madiba Essiben claims that the history of education under German colonial rule can be divided into two phases: phase one ran from 1884 to 1905 when it was promoted by missions. The second phase lasted from 1905 to 1914 when the German colonial administration began to provide education to train Africans for the administration and the commercial sector.[86] Government schools provided education aimed at instilling into the pupils German culture and civilisation using the German language. The curriculum comprised German Language, arithmetic, observation, geography, history and natural sciences.[87] School curriculums were prescribed by the German Education Law of 1910 which was abandoned when the First World War broke out in 1914. By 1913, there were four government schools in German Kamerun but none of these was in Bakunduland. Mbende of Supe was one of the few Bakundu who attended the government school at Kumba.

---

[85] Ibid.
[86] Ibid., 55.
[87] Ibid.

Table 13: The Primary School Timetable as Prescribed by the German Education law in 1910.

Class	Subjects	Hours per week	Total No. of Hours per Week
1	German	2	6 Hours
	Observation	2	
	Arithmetic	2	
2	German	3	8 Hours
	Observation	2	
	Arithmetic	3	
3	German	4	10 Hours
	Observation	2	
	Arithmetic	3	
	Geography	1	
4	German	4	10 Hours
	Arithmetic	3	
	History	1	
	Geography	1	
	Natural Sciences	1	

Source: Madiba Essiben cited by Martin Atinda "The Bakundu Under Colonial Rule, 1897 – 1961", University of Yaounde I, M. A. Thesis, 2006.

The German colonial government was not the only agent to spread Western education. Missionary societies were also involved. In Bakunduland, the Basel Mission led the way. From the very beginning, emphasis was laid on laying a foundation that would enable schools to help the people improve their living conditions. To this end, various kinds of schools were established to promote literacy so that every convert could read the Bible and to produce catechists, teachers and pastors for church congregations, as well as Christian clerks, traders and future leaders of the country.[88] For this purpose, the mission preferred the use of the native languages, like Duala as the medium of instruction in the schools of the coastal region and Mungaka in the Grass fields. *Idubwana Jombe* was the reading manual for Basel Mission schools in the coastal region.

Vernacular Schools

Initially, the Basel Mission built vernacular schools in some villages. By 1900, there were 131 and their popularity earned the name "schools for everybody".[89] Since many Bakundu villages had no school buildings, classes were held in church houses and in the compound of chiefs who were converts. Catechists also taught in these schools.[90] They were called vernacular schools because indigenous languages were used for instruction. The first Bakundu village to have a vernacular school was Bombe in 1898.[91]

Above the vernacular schools were the boy's schools and the middle schools. Until 1910, all these schools had one African and one European teacher and the language of instruction was German alongside the local languages. In 1902, a boy's school was opened at Bombe.[92] The school cycle lasted two years after which the brightest boys were sent to a middle school. Arithmetic, History, Geography, German, Religious Instruction and Manual Work were the subjects taught. In addition, a minor seminary was established at Bombe to train catechists. Unfortunately, the seminary was closed barely two years after its creation because a Catechist's Training Centre was opened in Buea in 1899 with Rev. Schuler as its first principal.[93] Of the three

---

[88] Keller, Brutsch and Schnellbach, *Presbyterian Church*, 20.
[89] Ibid.
[90] Ibid.
[91] Ibid, 21.
[92] Ibid.
[93] Ibid.

Bakundu children who were admitted, only one of them, Dikonge of Banga, completed the two year course.[94]

At the end of his course, Dikonge served as catechist in his village. He opened a farm to cultivate crops like cocoa using new agricultural techniques he learnt at the seminary. He provided lessons on agriculture to his kinsmen and built a new home with local materials which had a beautiful courtyard with flowers. He observed high standards of personal hygiene by ensuring that his animals were kept away from the house, and built a kitchen and a pit latrine away from the main house. He encouraged his people to send their children to school. He denounced witchcraft and made his people to understand its harmful social effects. He also taught them the educational value of travelling away from home. He once took one of his friends to Victoria, an experience which deeply influenced his friend's lifestyle, and changed his dressing and eating habits. His fight against "juju" practices led to open confrontation with the diehard juju men. He fought against them because in his view they were generally unprogressive and influenced many young people.[95]

"German Schools"

The Basel Mission also ran two other types of schools known as "German Schools" at Bonaberi and Bonanjo.[96] In these schools, priority was given to the study of the German language, in order to train boys who wanted to enter government service or serve with trading companies. The cycle lasted three years.[97] Bebe of Banga and Mbende of Supe were some of the Bakundu pupils who attended these schools. These were day schools and attendance was better perhaps because the boys were sure to find well-paid jobs

---

[94] Conversation with John Moki, Kake I, 7 March 2008.
[95] Conversation with Joseph Motuba, Buea, 26 February 2008.
[96] Keller, Brutsch and Schnellbach, *Presbyterian Church*, 22.
[97] Ibid.

when they completed their studies. Upon completion of the course Bebe and Mbende were employed by the colonial administration, the one as an interpreter and the other as a clerk.

Missionaries stressed the importance of manual labour and young Cameroonians were trained in various crafts: carpentry and smithing, while the girl's schools prepared them for domestic life as future mothers and housewives. Some girls were trained in the rudiments of domestic science by the wives of missionaries. These girls did not attend the girls' school. The girls from Bombe and Banga benefited most from this experiment since Bombe had resident missionaries. Two of the girls were Mariana Ete and Mary Basaka. They put into practice the lessons they learned in personal hygiene, always being neat, and always socialising with each other because they could not find other like-minded girls. They impressed the other girls in their village with their new skills. Their homes set the new standard of personal hygiene and home care that were taught by missionaries, providing further evidence of the beginnings of social distinction among Bakundu women. If nothing else, their new skills made them more desirable as wives and models in a changing Bakundu society. They did needlework and sewing. Through this, they were able to employ themselves. Their personal comportment in the village motivated other parents to send their daughters to be trained by the wives of missionaries.

Education and schools were not established to "encourage trade" but to provide at best literate and semi-literate clerks to serve European traders in managing their businesses, or the government in subordinate administrative functions. In this regard, the missionaries and the colonial government were partners.[98] First, they established schools, then gradually expanded them. Despite occasional disagreement, the missionaries and the government worked together to transform Bakundu society by first transforming individuals like Nathaniel Malomba Bebe of Banga.

Nathaniel Malomba Bebe
Bebe was born at Banga in 1894.[99] Like other families of Banga, his parents were poor people who lived a modest village life. At the age of ten he entered the vernacular school. His parents sent him to school not because they fully understood the implications of their decision, but simply because young Bebe was eager about the things of the Whiteman and wanted to know more about them. After two years he was transferred to the primary school. In 1908 he attended the German school at Bonaberi, Douala. At the end of his course, he worked as an interpreter to the Governor in Douala in 1911.[100] Three years later he stopped work when World War I broke out.

---

[98] For an enlightening discussion of education See Robert Redfield, *The Primitive World and Its Transformations* (Ithaca, New York: Cornell University Press, 1966), 120-121.
[99] Conversation with Bebe's daughter, Victoria Bebe, at Limbe on 16 August 2007.
[100] Conversation with Emmanuel Bebe at Banga on 10 November 2007. He is one of the surviving children of late Nathaniel Bebe who is now Chief of Banga.

Nathaniel Malomba Bebe

When the Germans left Cameroon after the First World War in 1914-1916, he was employed by the new British administration of Southern Cameroon mandate. He was posted to Nigeria where he worked in Lagos, Zaria, Calabar and Enugu successively. Because of his exemplary services he was Knighted with the Order of the British Empire (OBE). He worked for thirty-seven years before retiring to his native village of Banga.[101]

Using a loan he obtained from the British colonial government and his savings, he became involved in agriculture and trade. He opened banana, rubber and cocoa plantations at Banga and to encourage improved agricultural techniques, he donated a piece of land to the Department of Agriculture for research work.[102] He was the first Bakundu

---
[101] Conversation with Victoria Bebe, Banga, 8 November 2007.
[102] File No. 3221 Ca 1948, Kumba Division Annual and League of Nations Report, 1950, NAB.

man to ship bananas to Germany. Also, he grew food staples like yams and plantains, which he sold in bulk.

Bebe is said to have been a kind-hearted and generous man who came to the assistance of the needy. He lived a simple life, dressed Western and built the first modern house in his village. He was a very devoted Christian who hated witchcraft. Using the royalties obtained from a timber company operating in his village forests, he built the church house at Banga and equipped it with his own money. He warned his children never to associate with people who were suspected of witchcraft and he never joined any secret society.[103] He was thus a model of an emerging Bakundu elite.

His impact on Bakundu society is seen in the fact that many emulated his lifestyle and became interested in education, modern healthcare and personal hygiene, built modern homes and were generally progressive. He taught his children the ethic of being outspoken, honest and hardworking.[104] He is believed to be the greatest patriot of his time among the Bakundu.[105] Bebe's role in changing the lifestyles of many Bakundu was a direct result of his experiences gathered over the years working with the colonial governments. There is no doubt that his was a mission to promote change among his kinsmen by opposing unprogressive traditions. Thus he spent his life teaching them what it meant to adopt new ideas and modern ways. There is no doubt that some if not many of his people did not like him for the progressive ideas he championed. However, he was undeterred.

---

[103] Conversation with Bebe's daughter, Victoria Bebe, at Limbe on 16 August 2007.
[104] Ibid.
[105] Ibid.

Education Under British Rule

The British continued the German education policy which left the task of education in the hands of the missions. But in 1922, it was decided that most of the educational effort "in due course came under the direct control of Mission Societies who are in a better position than the administration to develop disciplined character".[106] This was so because the missions had already provided the structures and curriculum for the schools.

Most missionaries had left the territory as a result of the First World War but the Basel and the German Baptists continued with their programmes of education and evangelisation so that when the British arrived in Southern Cameroon in 1916, they found Basel Mission Schools in virtually all Bakundu villages.[107] The Mission at this time worked hand in hand with the British colonial government to expand educational opportunities among the Bakundu.

In his annual report on the state of education in the British Southern Cameroons, the Lieutenant Governor of the Southern Provinces of Nigeria, under which Southern Cameroons was administered, stated that all education of Cameroonians was in the hands of the Basel and Roman Catholic Missions.[108] The Roman Catholic Mission had big schools at Victoria, Buea, Ossing, Bikom and Kumbo. The Basel Mission, which also gave instruction in handicraft, had similar primary schools at Victoria, Bombe, Nyasoso, Besongabang and Bali. By 1924, the Basel Mission had a total of 32 primary schools.[109] In Bakunduland, it created a school at Itoki in the early 1920s which served children from

---

[106] Dundas and Carr. Reassessment Report on the Bakundu N.A.B.
[107] Ibid.
[108] Ibid.
[109] Ibid.

northern Bakundu villages of Mbu, Ibemi and Koba. Seven more schools were created in other villages subsequently.[110]

According to Dundas and Carr, between 1922 and 1926 the enrolments in the existing schools in Bakunduland was as shown in Table 14.

Table 14: School attendance in selected Bakundu Villages, 1922 to 1926.

Village	No. of Pupils
Kombone	40
Banga	40
Kombombo and Boa	20
Bole	30
Pete	30
Kake	25
Bopo	15
Ibemi	16
Itoki	25
Konye	20
Kokaka	10
Mbakwa	45
Ndoi	10

Source: Dundas and Carr, Reassessment Report on the Bakundu, N.A.B.

On 26 May 1926, a new School Ordinance came into force which authorised the government to supervise mission schools.[111] The schools were not up to the required standard because they lacked qualified teachers and infrastructure, and Lagos had to decide whether to approve or not approve them. With the intervention of the Resident at Buea, the Education Department permitted them to be registered as religious

---

[110] Conversation with Peter Ekoi, Kumba, 28 December 2007.
[111] Keller, Schnellbach and Brutsch, *Presbyterian* Church, 65

schools to teach reading, writing and religious instruction in the native tongue.[112]

Following seemingly endless appeals, the Education Department in Lagos recognised the religious schools as proper village schools. The schools and teachers were registered and supervised by the government. To solve the problem of unqualified teachers those pupils who passed an examination in English were recruited as teachers. Between 1926 and the early 1930s, the Basel Mission improved their old schools and created new ones.[113] Bakundu pupils who would later become teachers passed out of these schools in the 1930s, 1940s and 1950s.[114]

Among these were Marcus Efim Ebile, Peter Ekoi, David Mekumba, Peter Abene Obase and Ferdinand Mosaka. After their primary education, they enrolled in Teacher's Training Colleges like Government Teacher Training Centre in Kumba and the Presbyterian Teacher's Training Centre, Batibo in the 1940s and 1950s, where they earned the Teachers' Grade III, II and I certificates.[115] To encourage western education among the Bakundu, Marcus Ebile, Headmaster of Basel Mission School Dikume Balue, tried to form an association of Bakundu Basel Mission teachers in the late 1940s and 1950s. The attempt failed because of the dispersed nature of Bakundu villages and poor communication network. Still, the attempt was an indication of how much this generation of Bakundu had embraced Westernisation and how much they had become its agents, consciously or unconsciously. This failure did not discourage Ebile from advocating for the education of his people. To prod Basel Mission authorities act, Ebile wrote to the Supervisor of Basel Mission schools thus:

---

[112] Ibid., 65
[113] Ibid.
[114] Ibid.
[115] Conversation with Peter Ekoi at Kumba on 20 January 2008.

The Supervisor
Basel Mission Schools,
Southern Cameroons,
Buea.

AN APPEAL

Sir,

This letter is personal. It is a matter I have been contemplating about the entire tribe of Bakundu, from where I come. It is an appeal which needs careful considerations and not just a letter which needs a quick reply. I am lamenting over my beloved tribe. The matter I am going to appeal to you below, does not concern my work as a teacher in the above school; that is why I have not directed it through my Manager to you.

Educationally my tribe is in a predicament and unless this is gradually remedied it would have a poor stand in the succeeding generations on the side of our Church, in the tribe.

Excuse me to point it categorically that our Mother Church the Basel Mission, has not, in any wise, projected the tribe educationally for the better.

To start with during the advent of Swiss and German Missionaries into the Cameroons, we read that a Mission Station was built at Bombe-Bakundu as far back as 1897, and the first institution of higher learning then in the country was opened, "the Lower Middle School, Bombe". The Basel Mission Church ran through the whole tribe as magic and the natives embraced it wholeheartedly, and up to this era, there are no other Religious Denominations in such a large tribe. An extract from a book "Victoria – S. Cameroons 1858 – 1958" states, "It was the policy of the Basel Mission from the beginning to use Duala as the Church language and to train as many Cameroonians as possible for the ministry with the aim of building up a strong Church which would be entirely guided by them one day". Pastors and other church workers were trained by the Basel Mission. But from then up to 1954, this large tribe could not boast of any; the two Pastors – indigenes – were only ordained in 1955. Should I then believe that before this half-century, there were no Bakundus who could just read and write to take their place among others? Also, most of the high ranking men in the Basel Mission Schools, had their professional courses through the strong recommendations of the Mission. But this has never come across a Bakundu man's way. Some of them before the professional courses, had only the Grade Two Certificate. Some of our predecessors – the indigenes of the tribe, became disgruntled and had resigned from this employ.

Africa was scrambled and partitioned by Europe because of trade rivalry. I presume that if the tribe had embraced all religious denominations, educational attainment would have been competitive. Up till now, if the tribe cannot boast of men with high educational attainment through the efforts or the recommendation of the Basel Mission, how could we battle with other denominations which are trying to confuse the tribe?

Already, the Baptist and the Roman Catholic Missions, which were not in the tribe at first, are beginning to have tap roots. I, vehemently know that Swiss Diplomas and Degrees are very much valued in this country, is it impossible to have our people rewarded in this wise?

I humbly beg you, Sir, it is an appeal, not a challenge and needs consideration.[116]

I remain, yours faithfully
Marcus E. Ebile

The spirit of Ebile's petition is worth extended comment. He was concerned that the Bakundu were educationally disadvantaged compared with other ethnic groups in Kumba Division even though they are one of the largest groups. They had no Swiss diplomas and degree holders. Therefore, they were not progressing like the other peoples. While Ebile's petition reflects a secular and modernist attitude which instead helped the Basel Mission compete with other denominations like the Catholics and Baptist Churches, it also showed the disadvantaged position of the Bakundu at a time when other people were progressing in the kind of jobs they did and their contribution to the development of their area. Since the Bakundu had not acquired new skills the outcome was that Bakunduland lagged behind others. In this case, their failure to acquire Western education made them less competitive and therefore backward. Ebile saw this as an obstacle to Bakundu progress and therefore appealed to the Swiss Missionaries to aid by encouraging the Bakundu to acquire education. There seems to be no record of the Mission's response to this appeal. But it seems reasonable to assume the missions learned much about the thirst for the education among Bakundu children. This led to the education of a new generation that included men like Peter Ekoi.

---

[116] This later was written in June 1960 and is found in the Office of Manager of Presbyterian Schools, Meme Division, South West Region of Cameroon.

After independence people like Marcus Efim Ebile, Peter Abene Obase, Ndita Ngo and Johnson Ekole resigned from the Basel Mission and joined the government service. They were clearly in search of greener pastures – economic, financial and professional security which the government seemed to provide. Some of these former Basel Mission teachers excelled and rose to higher ranks as government teachers. Among them were Marcus Efim Ebile and Isaac Ndita Ngoh, both university graduates, who became principals of government secondary schools. Others were Ruth Ekole who was appointed Divisional Delegate of Nursery Schools in Ndian Division. Clearly, the Bakundu had come a long way in their ambiguous journey towards modernity. But much remained to be done.

Evangelism and Conversion
Evangelisation and conversion were the primary preoccupations of the missionaries but it was here that they had conflict with the people as a result of different worldviews. The Bakundu and other Africans look out upon the world with different eyes, interpret facts in a different way, not because they are constituted differently from European, but because they were taught to do so by their forefathers. These and other factors played a role in the Christianization of the Bakundu.

To aid understanding of the conversion process among the Bakundu, it is necessary to begin with a description of Bakundu cosmological ideas in order to show their compatibility or incompatibility with Christian western beliefs. These included the relation between man and his environment on which he depends, the belief in the ancestors who were seen as the intermediaries between the living and the dead. All of these continued Bakundu understanding and acceptance of new ideas directly and indirectly.

Africans did not see their traditional religious understanding as complete and unerring. As a result they were open to practices and beliefs from elsewhere that might come to individuals from the spirit world. Thus, at times, a ruler might adopt attractive new beliefs and practices to enhance his own powers. The new faith sometimes might become the official practice of his kingdom for all subjects.[117] This contributed to conversion.

The conventional Christian teaching of monotheism precluded ancestor veneration although in Bakunduland this did not. For Africans, this implied a potential rupture between the living and the dead, which was fundamental to their worldview. Some African religions are monotheistic because there is a single high God who created the world and humankind and he is the central source of order.[118] But many African religions are also polytheistic in that several gods or large number of spirits or ancestors, or some other kind of divinities stand between human beings and the ultimate deity. Rituals are / were part of all religions. Prayers were requested for health and well-being while sacrifices and rituals were used for cleansing and to provide avenues for communication between human beings and the deity.

Conversion might have been facilitated by a measure of mutual understanding that European and African cosmologies had much in common. For example, Iberian Christians accepted the existence of lesser spirits as angels and devils, of spiritually powerful intercessors such as saints, and the malevolent power of witchcraft, all of which had counterparts in African beliefs.[119] Because of these compatibilities, it seemed somehow easy for Africans to

---

[117] David Northrup, *Africa's Discovery of Europe, 1450-1850*. (New York, Oxford: Oxford University Press, 2002), 26-27.
[118] Bohannan and Curtin, *Africa*, 116.
[119] David Northrup, *Africa's Discovery of Europe, 1450-1850*. (New York, Oxford: Oxford University Press, 2002), 26-27.

grasp the essentials of Western Christianity and to adopt it as their own without abandoning everything of the old beliefs. Instead of being discarded, much of the old religion could readily be "converted" to the new ways. Thus, conversion consisted in conserving what remained valid of the old, adapting what needed to be redefined to include new elements. Thus, Christianity needed to be Africanized to be accessible to Africans as African beliefs and practices had to become Christianized.[120] This is a long-term process that required patience and mutual understanding.

To the African then, becoming Christian involved adapting Christian beliefs and practices to existing African beliefs and practices. To understand the process of conversion therefore requires an understanding of incoming messages on the indigenous religious frameworks and challenges they face from new experiences.

The missionaries took different approaches in converting the Bakundu to Christianity. First they preached a message of love and equality. This message appealed most to social groups like slaves, outcasts and the lowly in the Bakundu society because for the first time they were recognised and treated as human beings with the same rights as the other members of their communities. Gifts of European goods like textiles, mirrors and wrist watches, essentially "bribes", were sometimes used on people to entice them to the new religion.[121] Such methods are only one of the reasons why "conversion" is a difficult concept. It is possible that many early Bakundu converts were not converted from conviction but from such ulterior material interests.

---

[120] Ibid.
[121] Conversation with Ebenezar Obase, Kumba, 25 July 2007.

Bakundu Converts

One notable convert was Ndo Mbile of Mbu, a 'freeborn', in a village in northern Bakundu. A farmer and a hunter, had one wife and fathered seven children, and was a man of outstanding qualities like bravery. He was converted and abandoned secret societies. He became more tolerant, condemned witchcraft, and persuaded his family to become Christians and take advantage of Western education.[122] He always welcomed Basel missionaries to his home and wanted one of his sons to become a pastor. This dream was fulfilled when his nephew, Abel Modika, became a pastor in 1953. He also hoped that his daughters would marry pastors, a dream that was also fulfilled when his first daughter married Pastor Ekembe from Nyassoso.[123]

To show how much he valued the new faith and education, he expressed it in simple terms when he told Andrew Diongo that, "when you write a letter, you take it to the post office and drop it there. You do not see when the letter gets to its destination and after sometime, the reply comes; that is the best witchcraft, and not that which kills".[124] This was the testimony of a truly transformed life and worldview. Rare as it was, it is a measure of the depth or potential depth of change among Bakundu.

Another notable example of an early convert was Meshach Mbende from Supe. His conversion to Christianity is believed to have caused the "mysterious" death of all his children but one. Nevertheless, like Job in the Bible, he remained firm in his faith and crusaded against idol worship and witchcraft and encouraged others to follow his example and become Christians. In the absence of the village catechist, he often conducted Sunday service. Once, while he

---

[122] Conversation with Andrew Diongo, Douala, 20 September 2006.
[123] Ibid.
[124] Ibid.

was going to church he was chased by a 'juju' and a fight ensued. Other Christians joined and vowed to worship no other God. The story is told that at his burial at 7.00p.m., a beam of light shone over his grave and the presiding pastor, Hans Nkuge said, "this is a sign that this man of faith is accepted in heaven".[125] This "signs and wonders" approach to conversion inevitably impressed other people in a culture in which "signs and wonders" were an important aspect of the belief system and proof of "magical" ancestral intervention in daily life.

A person like Ndo Mbile of Mbu was asked to abandon his artefacts and totems which were objects of worship. Objects like carved statutes, potions and other traditional amulets worn round the waist in villages like Bombe, Nake, Kake, Mbu and Supe, were destroyed. Chiefs like Abia of Supe and Mosongo of Mbu were also prime targets for conversion, because it was believed that once they were converted, their subjects would follow them.

The conversion of slaves impacted Bakundu society. The Bakundu saw the transformation of their lives, first as they could understand and speak European languages, German and later English, and also saw them dress like Europeans.[126] Their children received the kind of training the children of the freeborn did not. This caused some of them to rethink their status. The Bakundu realised that if they did not become Christians, they would eventually be led by these men of influence, wealth and power.

Slaves received the gospel by attending church service or as they worked as church gardeners like Mathias Etongwe, a slave from the grass fields, at Bombe[127] who adopted a Bakundu name. Some of them were converted through their

---

[125] Interview with Ebenezar Obase at Kumba, on 25 July 2007.
[126] Ibid.
[127] Conversation with Joseph Motuba at Banga, 12 March 2008.

friends who were converted through contact with traders from other regions.[128] Another notable slave convert was Henry Modika of Bole who also wanted to be identified as a Bakundu. He died a few years after his conversion.[129]

Slavery implied that people lived in bondage and were not valued as human beings. This was true of Bakundu slaves. But in Biblical teaching, St. Paul did not say unequivocally that slavery was bad: thus, he merely advised Onesimus, a slave, to accommodate himself to it. Europeans engaged in the slave trade without qualms, and when they abolished it they did not do so primarily from 'Christian' principles but largely from economic interest.[130] To give slaves hope, dignity and a new lifestyle, the missionaries employed them as labourers in farms and domestic servants. The care and respect given to them by the missionaries confirmed the Christian message of love and equality.

Even more important was the change in the economic status of slaves. On the parcels of land they were given to grow their own food, they employed the new agricultural techniques they learnt from the missionaries. Naturally, they worked harder for themselves than they did for their former masters. For example, slave converts at Bombe produced more food than some freeborn and sold the surplus.[131] They had bigger harvests and earned more money than the freeborn. The outcome of these changes was a challenge to the age-old institution of household slavery.

The missionaries saw conversion as an individual's affair and thought it was impossible for converts to live in their old environment because they would be constantly tempted to revert to the old beliefs and ways. The missionaries therefore encouraged the new converts to build

---

[128] Conversation with Moses Ebollo at Kumba, 16 November 2007.
[129] Interview with Chief Nakomo, Kwakwa, 26 July 2007.
[130] Anene and Brown, *Africa*, 276.
[131] Chief Emmanuel Bebe to Joseph Ebune, Banga, 10 November 2007.

their homes close to the mission station where missionaries or catechists would supervise them. This supervision was intended to strengthen the converts in the new life and break them permanently from the old. It was a way to resocialise the converts, but it was difficult to maintain such a system in a period of large-scale conversion because of the limited numbers of church officials to supervise the new converts.[132] This seems to have been true of Bombe and other Bakundu villages as the numbers of converts increased.[133]

Role of Bakundu Catechists in Evangelisation

Catechists played a very significant role in the process of conversion because their changed lives were an inspiration and model for others. Abraham Nganda Nakomo of Mbu was a striking example.[134] Nganda served as a catechist with the Basel Mission in several congregations, and devoted his life to the service of his people and the church. An ascetic, Nganda literally believed in the heavenly rewards than in worldly ones.[135] He completed his primary education in Standard Four when his father died in 1940 and went to the Basel Mission Seminary at Nyasoso where he trained as a catechist for two years from 1946 to 1948.

He was against witchcraft practices and suffered persecution from members of secret societies who considered him a social misfit. In spite of this, he knew that the only way to win more converts was to be a friend to all. In his village of Mbu he visited all homes and educated people about happenings in the wider world. In the words of Reverend Emmanuel Sakwe, "Nganda was a real servant of God whose life reflected the teaching of the Bible. The values he lived

---

[132] Peil, *Consensus and Conflict*, 224.
[133] Interview with Rev. Namaya Elangwe, Buea, 16 August 2007.
[134] Conversation with Therese Nganda, Buea, 20 December 2007.
[135] Ibid., 90.

by influenced some of us to join the ministry".[136] His family life was an exemplary one; and he taught his four children to live an upright life and encouraged them to avoid polygamous marriage. He was a role model for many people in his village who changed from the old ways to the 'Christian' way of living.[137]

Andreas Mbela Mosina was another remarkable catechist. Like Nganda, after his primary school education he attended the seminary at Nyasoso. He married and had two children with the first wife before she died.[138] After some years he remarried. Mosina condemned idol worship and witchcraft and counselled people to adopt the new way of life particularly Western education. Mosina was so self-conscious that he never attended funerals of non-Christians.[139] Mosina's life and that of non-Christians seemed to clash with each other. The outcome was that two different types lived side by side.

There were thus two distinct communities living side by side in tense coexistence. The Christian community in Bakunduland was distinct from the village community. With the missionaries discouraging contacts with non-converts and any association with indigenous associations and their traditional lifestyle, the Christians had to perform their own communal labour without the assistance of the 'pagans'. They became more concerned with their own affairs like building churches, mission schools and housing for catechists. The same attitude was adopted when a mission

---

[136] Interview with Reverend Emmanuel Sakwe, Ibemi, 28 February 2008.
[137] Interview with Therese Nganda, Buea, 23 July 2007.
[138] Interview with Joan Namoango, Buea, 25 July 2007.
[139] Ibid.

station was opened at Itoki in the 1920s. The Christians only paid lip service to chiefs or openly disrespected them.[140]

This experience was instructive and many adopted a new life by accepting missionary teaching and the new values they introduced particularly formal education. One of them was David Nebonda Ekole whose daughter, Ruth Ekole, was one of the first girls to be trained as a teacher from Itoki. After her primary school education, she was employed as a pupil teacher by the Basel Mission. While working as a pupil teacher she was converted and decided to work for the church. She entered the Women's Teacher Training College, Mankon in 1963, and graduated in 1965 with a Teacher Grade III Certificate. She later obtained Teacher Grade II and I Certificates. But she eventually resigned from the Presbyterian Church and joined the government because the church's salaries were not competitive. She was posted to the Ministry of National Education and worked in the Inspectorate of Primary and Nursery Education in Yaounde and later won a scholarship to study in Britain and graduated with a Master's degree in nursery education. On her return home she became a government Inspector of Primary and Nursery Education.[141] Ruth Ekole summed up the influence of western education on her thus:

> When my parents sent me to school I did not expect so much especially as it was believed among my people that the place of a woman was in the kitchen. Studying together with boys in the same class and seeing that I was even doing better than some of them encouraged me to work harder. The end result of the attainment of western education has been the

---

[140] Paul N. Nkwi *Traditional Government and Social Change: A Study of the Political Institutions Among the Kom of the Cameroon Grassfields* (Fribourg: S. E. Friburgensia, 1976), 161.

[141] Interview with Ruth Ekole, Kumba, 17 March 2006.

independence I now enjoy as a liberated Bakundu woman as I am the master of my destiny deciding what I want to do and at what time. That I compete with my kinsmen in the achievement of my goal in life is the hallmark of western education. Even more interesting is the fact that my educational success especially among the Northern Bakundu destroyed the understanding that only boys should be educated, and today my success led to the desire by parents to see their daughters educated with the realisation that a girl's education is as important as that of a boy.[142]

Ekole's comment demystified the belief among the Bakundu that only boys could succeed in school, but proved that the education of both boys and girls was important. Ruth Ekole's Western education contributed to her partial alienation from Bakundu traditional culture. Her departure showed the church's inability to satisfy the people's secular needs meaning that there would be a time when perhaps many of its workers would abandon their jobs for those that would fetch them better salaries and wages. The outcome would be the church's failure in its secular vocation.

Another convert whose life was influenced by the church and western education was Johnson Ekole of Marumba I. After completing his primary schooling, he attended Presbyterian Teachers' Training Colleges at Nyasoso and Mankon and obtained a Teacher's Grade II Certificate. He later obtained a Teacher's Grade I Certificate through a competitive public examination. He taught with the Presbyterian Church and resigned after several years. In his own words:

---

[142] Ibid.

> Nothing can be more beneficial in life than the acquisition of knowledge and the fear of God. Education and Christianity have changed my life as I think not about myself but others. To others, the greatest thing I can give them is to bring enlightenment to them through teaching. That is why I stress education as life-changing. I believe that through thinking, man becomes creative and creativity brings productivity. This is why I spare no effort to teach my people the goodness in educating their children, in using their time productively, and above all the fear of God. These are lessons I will not stop teaching my people.[143]

These two experiences, one can argue, probably changed the minds of some Bakundu parents about Western education which was interrupted by the 1914-1916 World War.

Effects of the 1914 War

The outbreak of the War in 1914 temporarily halted the second phase of the missionary effort under German colonial rule. Many congregations were closed. In various Bakundu villages, secret societies revived with renewed strength. One of such places was Bombe. In March 1916, the Reverend Rohbe visited Bombe and was greatly disappointed to find that most of the congregations in the Balong and Bakundu area had ceased to function.[144] One of the few catechists in the Bombe district who had carried on with the work was Abel Mbong, the teacher at the vernacular school in Kumba about whom little is known.[145]

---

[143] Conversation with Johnson Ekole, Ekombe Three Corners, 1 July 2007.
[144] Keller, Schnellbach, Brutsch, *Prebyterian Church*, 48.
[145] Ibid.

Rohbe's visit encouraged three former pupils at Bombe - Itie Mukwelle, Itie Nanyinga and Masue Ndo - to resume the church work in the face of severe persecution. This persecution included threats to their lives if they continued preaching; people were urged not to help them in any way, a clear attempt to isolate them and perhaps make them recant their faith. It is believed that they never achieved more than a primary school education nor did their children achieve better education than their parents. But three times they rebuilt the church destroyed at Bombe by members of secret societies, and thus bore witness to the strength of their new faith.[146] The strength of their faith as seen enabled them to confront all forms of resistance against missionary work in Bakunduland.

The resistance to missionary work among the Bakundu was widespread everywhere. Broadly, this raises questions about the concept of resistance including religious, political and economic. Evangelisation contributed to the success of colonial rule by condemning traditional belief systems and African culture in general. Witchcraft was seen as an "irrational" belief which, rather than build a healthy society destroyed it with "false mystical" beliefs and practices. Chief Abia of Supe believes *"bolemba elema"*, meaning witchcraft is foolish because it wastes life and manpower. It is paradoxical that witchcraft is supposed to be the source of wealth of many relatively well-to-do Bakundu while men like Chief Abia see it as "foolish".

Although, there is no tangible evidence of how many Bakundu abandoned such practices, it is believed that mission teaching and preaching did much to wean some Bakundu from witchcraft to belief in God. From this perspective, the worship of spirits and ancestor veneration were now presumed to be ineffective and unproductive in

---

[146] Ibid., 49.

Bakundu society. The involvement of more Bakundu in trade, their adoption of improved agricultural techniques, and the increasing adoption of western medicine were some of the factors that moved the Bakundu towards modernity and improved the quality of life exemplified by people like Nathaniel Malomba Bebe of Banga. The initial resistance of the Bakundu to the missionaries subsequently gave way to acceptance of Western values when they realized these were in their interest.

Other Christian missions besides the Basel Mission operated in the Southern Cameroons. Though relatively late, Catholicism entered Southern Cameroons with the Pallotine Fathers on 25 October 1890.[147] The Pallotine Fathers began work among the Bakundu in places like Bole, Kombone Miso[148] and Kokaka in 1891. Like their Basel Mission counterparts, they worked relentlessly to convert the Bakundu to Catholicism, and emphasised improvement in agriculture, healthcare, hygiene and education.[149] Like the missionaries before them, they condemned all Bakundu culture which did not conform to their teaching and called on the people to abandon witchcraft and worship of spirits.

But the Catholics made relatively few converts, less than thirty, among the Bakundu. They built one school at Kombone Miso but no health facilities.[150] Their efforts at conversion did not lead to conflicts since the people were already aware of the new Christian teaching introduced by the Basel Mission.[151]

---

[147] Ngoh, *Cameroon*, 92.
[148] The main village is called Kombone which is inhabited by the Bakundu indigenes. The village now called Kombone Miso, meaning 'eyes' was a settlement which was created for the non-indigenes which the Catholic missionaries later named Kombone Mission.
[149] Atinda, "The Bakundu", 52.
[150] Interview with John Moki at Kake I on 7 March 2008.
[151] Atinda, "The Bakundu", 52.

The relationship between these Christian denominations deserves further comment. The rivalry, competition and cleavages between these religious communities played a role in changing the peoples' perception of Christianity. The churches disagreed among themselves over doctrinal issues and forms of worship. For example, the question of baptism by sprinkling versus immersion between the Basel Mission, later Presbyterians,[152] and the Baptists divided the Bakundu people. There were similar tensions over winning new converts.[153] For example, the Roman Catholic propaganda of "France is Roman Catholic, therefore the Cameroons have to be Catholic too"[154] created difficulties for the Protestants to operate successfully in French Cameroon especially in urban centres like Douala. When the German priests had to leave the country, at the outbreak of World War I, the Vatican quickly replaced them with Irish, French and Dutch priests, some of whom were sent to work in villages like Bole and Kombone Mission.[155]

These denominational tensions and divisions inevitably resulted in disagreements between the missions in Bakunduland and the colonial government.[156] These disagreements also brought about division among the Bakundu converts. For example, at Bole, sharp disagreements between Catholics and Basel Mission over doctrine and winning converts led to a split among the converts and non-converts who saw Christianity as a religion of confusion. Individuals and families had their own personal deities who acted as intermediaries between them and God or *Obase*. The missionaries' attempt to end such "superstitions"

---

[152] The name Presbyterians was adopted in 1957 when the Basel Mission in Cameroon gained independence from the Basel Mission in Switzerland.
[153] Keller, Schnellbach and Brutsch, *Presbyterian Church*, 49.
[154] Ibid.
[155] Conversation with John Nakomo, Kombone, 12 May 2007.
[156] Ibid.

inevitably led to tension and conflict in Bakunduland. To the Bakundu, such teaching disrespected their religious beliefs which also touched issues like the place of women in Bakundu traditional society.

In Bakunduland the religious differences were not always differences of fundamental theological issues as was the case in Europe but of mere form and ritual. Despite these differences and divisions, missionaries like Adolf Vielhauer, of the Basel Mission, E. Keller and Max Amann were united in the condemnation of African traditional religions and African culture, and worked relentlessly to induce Africans to accept Western values. At Itoki for example, sharp differences occurred between the converts and non-converts. Having adopted Western values, the converts tended to be contemptuous of other Bakundu non-Christians. They only socialised with each other and so isolated themselves from non-converts. It was only the wisdom of the missionaries that prevented open clashes which might have resulted in bloodshed and death.[157] This tendency has led Adu Boahen to observe that:

> By 1880 all the various activities of Christian missionary societies had had a profound impact on African societies. In the first place, the standard of living of the converts had changed, for some were wearing European-style clothes, had gained access to modern medicine, were living in houses built in modern style, were practicing monogamous marriage, and were feeling contemptuous of their own traditional institutions, their traditional polygamous system of marriage and their traditional religion.[158]

---

[157] Conversation with Abel Isoh, Kumba, 17 June 2007.
[158] Boahen, *African Perspectives*, 16.

What emerged from this substitution of old practices "with something new" is a form of religious syncretism that permitted the Bakundu and other Cameroon converts to have the best of both worlds. When the people took ill, for example, they recited prayers taught them in church and Sunday school by the missionaries of the Basel Mission, the pastor and/or the catechist. At best the words and formulas of these prayers were sometimes only superficially understood. However, when people felt really helpless, they turned to the traditional doctor or diviner with whom they shared a deeper emotional and social bond and who could be counted on to invoke the ancestral spirits to help find solutions to the deepest needs of his clients.

In the case of Bakundu, the outcome of this experience is that they began to adopt a more relaxed attitude to denominational differences. Thus, in the same family one could find Catholic, Baptist and Basel Mission Christians. Amongst the Bakundu one finds striking examples in the families of A. Nganda Nakomo of Mbu, Eric Dossa Sakwe of Banga, Pastor Ndo of Marumba Boa and Njemo Nebo of Ibemi. Although these people had played a role in the spread of the gospel in Bakunduland, no members of their families continued their work after them because they showed little interest in missionary work.

Pastors Njemo Nebo and Dossa are remembered as pious men. They were also so dedicated to their work that, like Nganda cited above, they paid little or no attention to material possessions. They raised their families on the meagre salaries paid by the church. They were tireless and each of them pastored several congregations. Education, they emphasised, was the only key to a better life, which is why they sent their children to mission schools. Though a Pastor, Njemo devoted his life to ensuring the wellbeing of his family. This attitude made him to be ruthless to less industrious people he considered living a wasteful life. As a result, he was feared so much that he was sometimes called a 'soldier of Christ'.[159]

In the respective villages, these men of God were regarded as threats to Bakundu tradition as they undermined their status, power and influence. Their sermons against witchcraft and idol worship earned them the wrath of members of these societies. To prove that these societies had no powers, Pastor Njemo dispersed a gathering of one society at Ibemi in Northern Bakundu, to the amazement of many villagers who expected him to die shortly afterwards. When he did not die as expected, many villagers in awe joined the church and became pillars in its evangelisation efforts.

There was no marked difference in the Christianisation of Northern and Southern Bakundu. The people's response to Christianity was largely the same. Dossa was a gentle and easy-going man. To him, the best life to live was a humble one based in "God's will". To avoid any confrontation with non-Christians, he kept much to himself and spent much time reading the Bible. He loved singing which attracted children and he taught children Duala songs. He lived a pious life and when he died many people believed that God received him in his Kingdom. In the face of overwhelming hostility, men like Dossa could not help but adopt a pietistic Christianity with its implication of withdrawal from society. In the course of time, however, missionaries and members of secret societies learned to live in an atmosphere of tolerance, which, ironically, some Western nations have only recently learned under the auspices of the Christian ecumenical movement,[160] which has broken the barriers between denominations as they all agree to worship the same God.

---

[159] Conversation with Jacob Lekendo, Kake I, 20 March 2008.
[160] Conversation with Henry Njemo, son of the late Pastor Njemo, Idenau, 16 January 2006.

Yet Christianity also brought doubts and uncertainties, adding a new dimension to social and spiritual life in Bakunduland that drove a wedge between religious and secular life. But the secret societies could no longer compete with the influence of missionaries who brought Western education and all its secular and modernising benefits.

Acceptance of Christianity among the Bakundu therefore begins with religion and the worldview based on it; with institutions like secret societies, polygamy and the extended family which are the very foundation of communal life and values in Bakunduland. To abandon these is to abandon one's dignity and self-worth. As stated earlier, the Bakundu believe in one God just as Christians do. Therefore, belief in a supreme deity, love for one's neighbour, the fulfilment of people's economic and social needs were common in Christian and Bakundu belief systems. In view of this, the Bakundu saw Christianity as similar to what they believed was essential for happy living. Since Christian teaching did not seem to differ much from what they knew was good for them, the Bakundu who had earlier resisted the missionaries accepted it believing that it would improve their personal well-being.

There were conflicts between the two value systems. The conflict with African communal values began with the missionary emphasis on the conversion of the individual. This had enormous socio-psychological implications for the individual and the community, especially for institutions like family and marriage and kinship upon which the Bakundu society was based. Once an individual was converted, he or she tended to isolate himself or herself from non-converts. This led to alienation and loneliness. The resulting tension and crisis of identity was often painful and confusing. By 1898 the station at Bombe and its out-stations had 130 Christians and 174 catechumens. That same year new converts were made in the rest of Bakundu area as shown in Table 15.[161]

Table 15: Number of convert in Bakundu Area in 1898.

Village	No. of Christians	No. of Catechumens
Bombe	20	24
Kake	17	21
Bole	13	20
Boa	09	16
Banga	16	23
Ndifo	06	17
Konye	14	14
Mbakwa	17	13
Ibemi	05	11
Itoki	07	10
Mbu	06	05
Total	**130**	**174**

Source: Nyansako-ni-Nku, *The Pioneers, A Century Picture Book*, 1886 – 1986, 34.

It is not easy to draw any conclusions about the percentage of Bakundu Christian converts from these figures because of the lack of census figures for Bakundu villages for 1898. As a result, whatever inferences can be made are only tentative. However, one can argue that conversion was slow and limited because people first had to study the new religion to see how compatible it was with their belief systems and customs. This cautious attitude is understandable in view not only of the foreign language in which the gospel was transmitted but also of the strange men who acted as its agents.

---

[161] Nyansako-ni-Nku cited by Atinda "The Bakundu", 52.

Marriage, Family and Society

Christian doctrine, Catholic or Protestant, held different fundamental beliefs and social ideals from those of the Bakundu and other Africans. One of these was about marriage and family. Everyone was expected to get married since this was important for the community. The economic factor also played a part. Agrarian societies require a large number of hands to contribute to economic well-being of the community. This necessitated more than one wife. On the other hand, high mortality rates especially among male children required that those who survived take more than one wife. Also, permitting men to have more than one wife made it possible for a widow and her children to be looked after as the brother of the deceased was expected to look after the widow and her orphaned children. On the other hand, the desire to have an heir to carry the family name allowed for polygyny. Instead of divorcing a barren wife, the husband was allowed to take another wife.

The missionary teaching about marriage and family centred on monogamy as the best form of marriage. For this reason, the European missionary from an individualist society found the African family system not only odd, but a negation of some of the things he considered most vital in life, including not only monogamous marriage, but also the freedom of worship and the responsibility of each adult to God for his own soul.[162] The Africans defended polygamy but the missionaries responded simply by quoting the church's teaching on monogamy as God's only sanctioned form of marriage.[163] The African defense of polygamy is echoed by Hodgkin who notes:

> But in general, while polygamy tends to be more tolerantly regarded in independent than

---

[162] Ajayi *Christian Missions*, 15
[163] Khapoya, *African Experience*, 157.

in Mission Churches, this is essentially one aspect of the broader separatist principle – that Christian ethics, as commonly understood in Western Europe, must be adapted to the African tradition and social setting; and those elements in Mission teaching which derive primarily from European customs discarded. As a Nigerian pamphleteer, somewhat naively argue: "In England [polygamy] is regarded as an offence against the state. I dare suggest reasons for this. The English woman is very jealous of love and does not like to share her husband's love with another. Our women are not like this…." Monogamy is thus frequently regarded not as a Christian, but a European institution, lacking scriptural sanction ….[164]

Khapoya explains the rationale for polygyny marriages in Africa. Marrying multiple wives is commonly found all over Africa. The age-old custom is consistent in the social structure of traditional agrarian society and its rationale is rooted in the people's experience. Polygyny raises the social status of the family concerned. Extended families therefore meant greater social prestige.[165]

These are only a few of the reasons why polygamous marriages were contracted in Bakunduland as elsewhere in Africa.[166] Although these were the main reasons for contracting such marriages, in Bakunduland, the desire for prestige seemed more important.

Polygamous marriages before and during colonial rule were not without problems. These were problems of jealousy and rivalry. Quarrels often broke out amongst the wives and

---

[164] Thomas Hodgkin., *Nationalism in Colonial Africa* (New York: University Press, 1968), 103.
[165] Khapoya, *African*, 33-36.
[166] Ibid.

children on issues of right of inheritance of property and succession. These and many more are the disadvantages of polygamous marriages, which the missionaries tried but failed to suppress by encouraging monogamy.

The condemnation of polygamous marriages among the Bakundu bred a lot of ill will against the missionaries. Despite this, polygamists like Elias Mosima and Obase Nakeli from Supe became Christians. These two were only a few of the men who had more than one wife.[167] They took part in all church activities but were not communicants because the church forbade polygamy.

Women in Bakundu Society
The whole question of the repression and domination of women is a complex and controversial one. As feminist studies are now revealing, this has been largely misunderstood and we are now beginning to learn more about the status and rights of Bakundu women in traditional society which were undermined under colonialism.

One cause of such tension was the status of Bakundu women. Women, for example, were traditionally subject to men and were regarded as their property. Bakundu women had no control over their sexuality, and did not own property. The Christian message of equality appealed to the womenfolk because it promised liberation. The missionaries were conscious of one thing: that the Bakundu and other Africans would never be Christianised until the women were converted and liberated from male domination. Their repression called for relief.[168] The quest for relief together with the new awareness of being recognised as human beings more or less with "equal rights" made many Bakundu women

---

[167] Conversation with Ebenezar Obase, Buea, 20 July 2007.
[168] Edwin W. Smith, The Christian Mission in Africa: A Study Based on the Work of the International Conference at Le Zoute, Belgium, September 14th to 21st, 1926, 45.

to accept the new teaching.[169] According to Joan Namowango, a Bakundu woman's role in a family was limited to child-bearing and taking care of the home.[170] Among those who were converted were Mariana Ete of Marumba and Ngonde Isokwe of Banga, who in turn persuaded their husbands to become Christians.[171] In such ways, slowly but surely, women contributed to the work of evangelisation, to their own liberation and ultimately to change of attitude by Bakundu men. In other words, women ceased to be only victims and became agents of change in creating the new society with new values.

The Christian teaching that women were equal to men in all respects was resisted by men. The men did not accept it because it undermined their control over women. Although records are lacking for Bakunduland to show women's response to this new teaching, one can only suppose that the men became even more severe on those women who tried to claim and exercise their rights in the face of men's protest. The Bakundu proverb, *miayari ma mwalana ma sa tombaka mokoko* (when a woman urinates her urine never goes further than that of a man), indicates male evaluation of women. No matter what a woman did, however intelligent she might be or what professional status she achieved or her family background, she could never be a man's equal in Bakunduland.

Without doubt, African women suffered a lot of disabilities including polygamous marriages: men's attitude towards them and the fact that they were considered men's property under the bridewealth regime are only the most obvious. All of this gave them low social status in society, and low self-esteem. Polygamous marriages have reduced the

---

[169] Interview with Joan Namowango, Buea, 15 August 2007.
[170] Ibid.
[171] Conversation with Joseph Maloba, Buea, 5 May 2006.

importance and the power of some women. Senior wives had more powers than the junior wives. Sometimes the children of one wife were favoured which led to increased jealousy and tension. This happened because in some cases, it was not possible for a man to spread his affection and attention equally to multiple wives and children, and potentially unlimited number of people who had equal kinship claims on him. In other words, the usual problems of monogamy were or could be multiplied several fold, depending on the ethos at the particular home. Consequently, a woman could not stop a man from marrying another wife if he so pleased. Because the women had no choice they suffered all sorts of real or fancied slights.

Men did not treat women publicly as equals and only occasionally allowed them a role in making family decisions. In most cases, the women accepted rather than judge a man's decision. The status of the woman in the family was thus limited to the gendered roles of raising children, looking after the home and generally to domesticity. Women were excluded from rituals except initiation in *Maloba*, a women's cult which prepared the young for adulthood. Initiation was a ritualised teaching of the initiates that women must stand behind and support men.[172] They were not members of men's associations and were forbidden to eat certain foods like chicken and eggs. In this view, the woman was not an equal of a man. Still, women also had their own "spheres" like childbirth which involved rituals and women's associations like *maloba* from which men were excluded.[173]

Because a man paid the bridewealth to the wife's family, she was considered his personal property; he owned her. The woman had no right over herself and for this reason had to depend on a husband's orders and do his bidding. In

---
[172] Ibid.
[173] Ibid.

case of divorce, the bridewealth had to be returned. In this respect, her rights were greatly curtailed.

Missionary and Western attitudes towards the extended family were at odds with the family values and the kinship structure of Africans who shared a common ancestry. The extended family is a larger social unit and includes more blood relatives than the nuclear family in the Western world.[174] In extended families, three or more generations of blood relatives live side by side intimately - grandparents, uncles, aunts, nephews and nieces - working together for the common good. The extended family system seemed to fit nicely into the African communal ethic and pattern of life. It had its positive and negative aspects, depending on one's point of view.

Among the Bakundu and other Africans, such large families are highly valued. Children are prized because they perpetuate the family name and continued the blood line, the social values and norms handed down by ancestors. Children belong to the parents and to the community of relatives. It was common for children to be sent to live with relatives in other villages for years without their uterine parents worrying about how they were being raised. This was an indication of the harmony and trust due to the communal ethos. In the past this practice served to strengthen kinship ties.[175]

The missionary family ideal was based on monogamy. This missionary ideal of family was at odds with that of the Bakundu. But to the Bakundu and other Africans, marriage is vital and social institution of prime importance, linked to reproduction and survival of the community. Having children is an important contribution which each individual is expected to make to his/her society and one way of ensuring this was the institution of polygamy. The greater the number

---

[174] Khapoya, *Africa.*, 48.
[175] Ibid., 49.

of children the higher the person's status. Society recognises that contribution by elevating the status of a married person above that of an unmarried one.[176] Its condemnation by missionaries was seen as total disregard for African values and was resisted by the Bakundu.

Conclusion

The nineteenth-century Missionary movement provided additional ideological support for the new imperialism in Africa. The biblical command "to go into the world, and preach the gospel..." was literally taken up by Protestant men and women as they went abroad from their homes, cultures and societies to preach the word through evangelisation and conversion to Christianity.[177]

To the Christian missionaries, discipleship was not experienced in isolation. The Christian Missionary in Africa looked to the formation of a Christian society in which men and women could live in corporate worship, fellowship and service. But the missionaries failed especially to understand the social ideas and ideals of the Bakundu including polytheism, polygamy and the extended family and secret societies which they condemned. Bakundu acceptance of Christianity did not mean that they ceased to be Africans. They still observed their ancestral ways as required by their tradition and customs in order to maintain a link between the living and the dead. In this way, continuity was only partly broken. Nevertheless, they were frequently torn between being Christians and being faithful to ancestral ways.

In the colonial conquest even though the colonial government determined the policies, there was ample room for cooperation and division of labour between government and Missions, – church and colonial state – which is why

---

[176] Ibid., 30.
[177] Goucher, LeGuin and Walton, *Global History*, 736.

government subsidised mission schools. In the early days, not many Bakundu were interested in formal schooling for their children who traditionally were expected to help their parents as farm labour that was considered more gainful than learning to read. Two systems of education therefore operated in Bakunduland as elsewhere in Africa – the Bakundu traditional and western systems. The importance of traditional education cannot be overemphasised as it helped to preserve and transmit indigenous culture from one generation to another, while the western system introduced new values, stimulated innovation and change thereby expanding people's horizons and enabling them to cope with the challenges of modernity. As President Nyerere of Tanzania once observed, education helps to transmit from one generation to the next the accumulated wisdom and knowledge of society and helps to politicise future citizens who would lead the drive for the development of their societies.[178]

The popular view of tradition as associated with rural, agrarian, pre-scientific values and a corresponding resistance to change and innovation while modernity is considered scientific, rational, innovative and future-oriented is simplistic and largely erroneous.[179] The process of change is more complex and tradition and modernity worked simultaneously in Bakunduland after the introduction of Christianity and western education because change did not mean a radical break with the past. Rather, it was a process of adaptation and adjustment. The Bakundu did not forget the old ways. The ancestors were still venerated. In this view, there was potential harmony or clash between the old and the new ways.

---

[178] Peil, *Consensus and Conflicts*, 176.
[179] Kwame Gyekye, *Tradition and Modernity: Philosophical Reflections on the African Experience* (New York: Oxford University Press, 1997), 217.

As a result, the transition from tradition to modernity can be likened to a journey full of uncertainty. Like all Africans, the Bakundu did not know exactly where they were going, yet they realised they were going somewhere. And like all Africans their journey was an ambiguous one. Along the way, they chose what they considered useful. To cite only one example, traditional titles and honours, which might be considered outdated by some, continue to be valued today by educated Bakundu, and these same educated Bakundu continue to covet chieftaincy titles and want to join secret societies to enhance personal advancement and status. In this way they become, so to speak, modernizers in their societies, a status that is not easy to negotiate. What emerges from this coexistence of old and new is neither total acceptance nor total rejection but a compromise between the two in the creation of a "new society" in which modernity and tradition each play a transformative role in Bakundu society, especially in its secular dimension.

CHAPTER FOUR
NEW SOCIAL FORMS, AGENCIES AND ORIENTATIONS

Introduction

The overall nature, direction and pace of change in Bakunduland were determined by the colonial government policy and initiatives within the framework of Indirect Rule. Thus, in addition to the missionary activity discussed in the last chapter, there were non-missionary sources of secular change among the Bakundu, foremost among them education and politics.

Education and Modernisation

Formal education under German colonial rule, based on the German Education Law of 1910, has already been discussed above. Here the discussion is limited to British colonial policy and practice. Education, defined here as formal schooling and broad experience of the wider world created a new dynamic for politics, economics and social relations. Under British rule, "informal" Bakundu tradition was modified through modern education but its core values like extended family and kinship were only partly or imperfectly replaced by Western schooling. It created a new elite, with the skills of reading, writing and arithmetic and filled them for new employment opportunities and a new status and source of wealth and well-being. Here as elsewhere in Africa, this new social group comprising civil servants, teachers, ex-servicemen, plantation workers, professionals and intellectuals could be named the "colonial elite" or "colonial bourgeoisie". British colonial policy, practice and motives were best reflected in the transformation of indigenous society. Thus, in political memoranda of Lord Lugard, it was designed to train "promising" boys as native court clerks, school teachers in rural areas. Lugard was a colonial official who served in Uganda and later in Nigeria. It was his experience in Northern Nigeria that led him to formulate his perspective on indirect rule. In 1922 he published a book, *Dual Mandate in Tropical Africa*, which outlined his ideas for colonial administration in considerable detail. The text became a statement of policy for British colonial rule in Africa.[180] In Lugard's view:

> The primary function of education should in my judgement be to fit the ordinary individual to fill a useful part in the environment with happiness to himself and to ensure that the exceptional individual shall use his abilities for the advancement of the community and not to its detriment or to the subversion of constituted authority.[181]

It was a conservative policy, designed to disrupt the status quo as little as possible to transform society gradually not radically by inculcating new values. Also, the new educational system was to encourage obedience to established African authority under colonial supervision. This gave birth to Indirect Rule which was paternalistic. It sought to maintain indigenous institutions provided they were not "repugnant" to British and "Christian" moral standards and promoted the economic interests of colonizers.

Institutionally, the British promoted Western education through Native Authority (N.A.) schools. The first of these schools were created in the Southern Cameroons in 1922. The schools were limited to the primary cycle and served as "feeders" to the urban and semi-urban schools. There were ten in number with a total enrolment of 843 pupils. This number rose to fourteen in 1930, to eighteen in

---

[180] Erik Gilbert, Jonathan T. Reynolds, *Africa*, 290.
[181] Cited by Nkwi, *Traditional Government,* 165.

1935 and nineteen in 1937.[182] Of the six schools in Kumba division, two were found in Southern Bakundu, at Banga and Kombone Bakundu where prominent Bakundu elite like Joseph Njibili, Moses Ebollo, Emmanuel Lokendo and Christy Beseka studied. Because there was none in northern Bakundu, northern Bakundu children attended the N.A. school at Kurume. Located mainly in rural areas, their main goal was to adapt the children to a better rural lifestyle.[183]

To make the schools more effective, the government appointed indigenes as head teachers and Superintendent to conduct regular inspection tours to ensure improved teaching.[184] All schools in Southern Bakundu had infant and elementary cycles. British colonial education brought opportunities for self-advancement for all classes of people. It brought awareness to the people on how to profitably use one's time, how to earn a living through petty trade or wage labour or improved agriculture. Even more important was the fact that people came to learn new things like new dress codes.

The New Class
This initial resistance to Western education among members of secret societies and other Bakundu had far-reaching consequences. It sought to protect Bakundu cultural values by preventing children from attending school. However, it unknowingly gave underprivileged children a head start in education and eventually privileged them in the emerging new society. In this new society, it is such children who were employed as teachers, clerks, interpreters and also played a leading role in petty trade. Their social status changed accordingly and enabled them to interact more directly with

---
[182] Jacob A. Ihims, *A Century of Western Education in Cameroon: A Study of its History and Administration (1844 – 1961)*, (Bamenda: Unique Printers, 2003), 40.
[183] Ibid.
[184] Ibid, 40-41.

the colonial authorities than the children of the traditional elite. This upward social mobility involved them, collaboration with the colonial authorities, in decision-making that affected the Bakundu society. The slaves and lower classes were not the only ones to achieve this upward mobility.

Other Bakundu who were Westernised or semi-Westernised became modestly prosperous materially rose in social status and prestige. They became the object of jealousy, envy and witchcraft accusations. Men like Mbende of Supe and Bebe of Banga accepted Western values while others worked hard to preserve traditional values.[185] Others like Etoto of Supe and Mbile, often considered social deviants and a threat to traditional order, were always not accepted in the circles of those who clung to tradition, and were looked upon as agents of the Whiteman sent to destroy and disrupt the social fabric. In spite all these, those Bakundu who had embraced Western values blended them with the traditional ways of life.

The acquisition of Western education did not completely alter the Bakundu way of life. The educated still clung to those traditional occupations like farming. That is why those Bakundu like Elangwe who achieved status and economic security through the public service as a minister, nevertheless continued to farm. Farming provided / provides a bond between the Bakundu and the soil. Their traditional status is deeply bound in it. But they skilfully maintained their new status with one foot in tradition and the other in modernity thanks to their education. As a result, many of these modernisers owned large cocoa farms and cultivated food staples like plantains and cocoyams and sometimes sold the surplus. Joseph Maloba, a teacher, noted that this was a source of additional income and was a lesson to their less

---

[185] Conservation with Chief Samuel Ndome, Kake II, 10 July 2007.

Westernised kinsmen, a lesson in more productive use of land as a source of economic security.[186] On the other hand, Chief Samuel Mukwele Ndome, a teacher, from Kake II, pointed out that when he retired farming was the only thing on which he could depend for his livelihood. Moreover, as a traditional ruler, land meant even more to him because:

> To a Bakundu, land is where life begins and ends. It is the strength of our existence and the basis of all our livelihood. It is the meeting point of the living and the dead, the joy and the sorrow of our people. It is the hope of our lives which extends even to the unborn child. We till the land and it is through it that we invoke the spirits of our ancestors. It is through it that we commune with them as we tell the ancestors what we want. What we yield from the land is the answer to our petitions. That is what the land means to a Bakundu and anyone who stays away from it is a dead person. Therefore, to live means we till the soil.[187]

Such people who had acquired western education which changed their traditional outlook impacted their society by helping to introduce new things to enable their people move along with the times. In this way, they would compete with other people to attain a new standard of life. Nevertheless, these people still maintained their traditional values. They blended tradition and modernity. Other modernisers like Johnson Ekole of Marumba I combined teaching with petty trade. Ekole realised that his monthly salary as a teacher was not enough to help him meet the needs of his nuclear and extended family. He invested in petty trade. As costly as the business turned out to be, the proceeds

---

[186] Conversation with Joseph Maloba, Buea, 27 July 2007.
[187] Conversation with Chief S. M. Ndome, Kake II, 27 July 2007.

from his provisions store earned him more money not only to educate his family; but his success became an object lesson to other Bakundu civil servants who realised that frugality, hard work and prudent use of one's resources are the key to a higher standard of living.[188]

Naturally, these men were the first to realise that the Bakundu had to compete with other ethnic groups in all spheres of national development, which is why they spoke out against traditional values which they considered unprogressive. Echoing the missionaries, Peter Ekoi of Itoki launched a personal crusade not only against witchcraft and juju practices, but also against early marriages.[189] Their efforts touched on the fundamental aspects of change – intellectual, psychological and cultural. They were essentially new men with new values and a new outlook on life.

Their modern outlook is evidenced by the fact that they built modern residences in towns like Kumba, Mbonge, Muyuka, Tiko and Victoria in which they lived. Villagers visiting these towns saw and emulated their example.[190] Other Bakundu like Ebile, Motuba and Chief Rudolf Itoe owned bicycles, gramophones, radios and cars and modern dress, diet and personal hygiene made them role models in the society. In the same spirit, men like Motuba of Kake I, Bebe of Banga, Mediko of Konye and Ituka of Wone who owned farms built cocoa drying ovens. In all these ways and activities, these men and women distinguished themselves as precursors and agents of modernisation. The new class of Bakundu – teachers, clerks, interpreters, catechists, pastors and plantation workers –formed an association, the Bakundu Improvement Union in the late 1930s and 1942 which did not

---

[188] Conversation with Johnson Ekole, Ekombe, 27 July 2007.
[189] Interview with Peter Ekoi, Kumba, 26 July 2007.
[190] Ibid.

achieve much initially. This initial effort did not succeed because the new Bakundu elite had not understood its importance.

Among all these new Bakundu, teachers held pride of place in society. They could be easily identified, for example, by the fountain pens they wore in pockets of their shirts, or the hose they wore, their manner of speaking and general comportment. According to Joseph Maloba, a teacher from Banga, teachers were village letter writers, interpreters of government texts, and advisers to the village traditional councils as well as errand boys. They represented the village in meetings convened by the colonial authorities, were counsellors and for those who were Christians, lay preachers in the village congregations and an omnipresent model.[191]

There is, however, a negative side to this popularity of teachers. While people of other ethnic groups encouraged their children to attend technical and secondary grammar schools to learn trades, most Bakundu teachers sent their children to teacher training colleges many of whom, upon completion of their training, did not aspire to anything else. As a result, the Bakundu could not compete with other ethnic groups in other fields of endeavour because they did not have the required technical skills.

Thus the model of success or progress represented by these men as one generation of Bakundu teachers followed the other was conservative model. So popular was it that even when these men retired from active service they continued to be addressed as "teacher" in their community or in some cases by the more prestigious title "H.M." for "Headmaster".

Between 1940 and 1950, the colonial government, the N.As and the missions expanded educational opportunities by opening elementary training centres to train teachers for the elementary schools and also encouraged technical

---

[191] Conversation with Joseph Maloba, Buea, 26 January 2008.

education by opening a Trade Centre at Ombe[192] where subjects like cabinet-making, woodwork, painting, welding and metal works and mechanical trades were taught. On the other hand, the Cameroon Development Corporation (CDC) also opened schools for the children of the workers in the plantations.

Within this period, other Bakundu boys like Peter Motoko Molongwe, Ebenezar Namata Ewanga, Adolf Nyangwe, Benjamin Itoe, Welensky Etinge and Rudolf Duala Itoe studied in post-primary institutions in Nigeria sponsored by government or their families. Among these, Ebenezar Namata Ewanga won a scholarship from the Southern Cameroons government to study in Nigeria and the United States of America in the 1960s.

Ebenezar Namata Ewanga

After graduating from the Yaba College of Technology in June 1962 with a Higher National Diploma in Architecture, Ewanga proceeded to the United States of America in October 1963 and obtained a B.A. and an M.Sc

---

[192] Ihims, *A Century of Western Education*, 75.

in Architecture from the University of Kansas in 1968. On his return home he worked with the Ministry of Housing and Town Planning until 1973, but later resigned and established a successful architectural firm, Namata Ewanga Associates in 1972.

His political career began in 1980 when he was elected member of the Meme Cameroon National Union (CNU) Section executive. When in 1985 the Cameroon Peoples' Democratic Movement (CPDM) replaced the Cameroon National Union (CNU), he became the Section President of Meme Division. Following further reorganisation of the Meme Section which was split into three sub-sections, he became the president of Konye sub-section. In 1997 he represented Meme-West constituency in the National Assembly, and was appointed member of the Central Committee of the ruling CPDM party. According to Ewanga, Bakundu society was changing towards modernity and he clearly saw himself as a moderniser when he noted that:

> The coming of the Europeans into Bakunduland had profound effect on my people in the fields of economics, politics and culture. The society moved fast towards modernity following the changes introduced first by missionaries and later colonial administrators. This is why our people embraced the new economic system, the whiteman's laws and a new lifestyle in order to keep abreast with these changes although not without difficulties which were overcome with time. As far as I am concerned my experience is that these changes are continuing up till this day as we copy, or borrow from other ethnic groups changes taking place among them. The fact that we interact, and exchange ideas has even done more to our people. No doubt, then,

our economy has improved with the growing of cash crops like cocoa. Socially we are abreast with the times and even in national politics, our people have raised sons and daughters who have made significant contributions in the growth of the Cameroon society. I know, I have also done much to modernise my society, especially in the field of education by helping many young Bakundu who could not without this help pursue their goals of education.[193]

Namata Ewanga, a Northern Bakundu from Konye represents the post-independence generation of politicians. There is a difference in Elangwe and Ewanga's political experiences. The difference between them is that Ewanga did not hold a cabinet post in the Cameroon government although his position as section president of the Cameroon Peoples' Democratic Movement (CPDM) and member of the Cameroon National Assembly made him a potential power broker. That in itself was an achievement.

Ewanga's significance, like that of other Bakundu such as Benjamin Itoe and Chief Henry Namata Elangwe lies in the inspiration they gave the younger generation to pursue higher education. His contribution to society has been his support of the less fortunate Bakundu to acquire education.[194]

Bakundu and National Politics

It is a mark of Bakundu progress when educated men like Ewanga felt comfortable enough to take the plunge into national politics. The best example is Namata Elangwe, now an octogenarian. Elangwe's political career began in Nigeria where many Southern Cameroonians went to study due to

---

[193] Conversation with Namata Ewanga, Limbe, 15 December 2007.
[194] Ibid.

lack of educational institutions in Southern Cameroons. He participated in the pre-independence struggle together with people like E.M.L. Endeley, N.N. Mbile, J.N. Foncha, S.T. Muna and P.M. Kale.[195]

These men were pioneers in nationalist politics who raised political consciousness among Southern Cameroonians first by forming pressure groups that called for the creation of a region for Southern Cameroons like other Nigerian regions. People like Endeley and Kale helped to form the National Council of Nigeria and the Cameroons (NCNC) led by Dr. Nnamdi Azikiwe. They formed political parties. Political parties in Southern Cameroons owed their origin to the Eastern Regional Crisis at Enugu between Dr. Nnamdi Azikiwe, leader of the NCNC and Eyo-Ita, the regional leader who disagreed over the question of ministerial posts in the Eastern and Central Houses. A clash of authority developed between Azikiwe and his supporters on the one hand and Eyo-Ita and his supporters on the other. The thirteen Southern Cameroon representatives came to allay with Azikiwe's NCNC faction. Unfortunately, despite Azikiwe's positive declaration, the Cameroonians being in the minority were defeated again in their demand for a separate Southern Cameroon's region. This caused the Cameroonians to form a neutral block in the Eastern Regional House.[196] They decided to walk out of the House and to boycott all future elections into the Eastern Regional House because the NCNC paid no attention to the demands of Southern Cameroonians.

As further protest to this legislative situation, the thirteen representatives called on all Southern Cameroonians to send two representatives from each section of the territory to a general conference to be held in Mamfe from 22 – 23

---

[195] Ibid.
[196] Ebune, *Political Parties*, 139.

May, 1953 to fight for their own House of Assembly. One of the resolutions of the Mamfe Conference was to create a political party that would fight for the future of Southern Cameroon. It was then agreed that Endeley's Cameroon National Federation (CNF) and R.J.K. Dibonge's Kamerun United National Congress (KUNC) merge to create the first political party, the Kamerun National Congress (KNC) with its motto "Towards self-government or independence for a United Cameroon".[197]

In June 1953, a second political party, the Kamerun People's Party (KPP), with its desire to fight for regional autonomy for the Cameroons and secession from Nigeria was founded by N.N. Mbile. It was also to act as an opposition party in parliament in conformity with democratic principles of government. In August 1955, John Ngu Foncha broke away from the KNC and formed the Kamerun National Democratic Party (KNDP) because Endeley failed to adhere to the original party programme of reunification of the two Cameroons.[198]

On the other hand, Benjamin Itoe, a Southern Bakundu from Bombe, is a second generation bureaucrat-politician. He became involved in politics not as Elangwe did in party machinery but through the civil service.

---

[197] Ibid., 142.
[198] Ibid.,

Chief Justice Benjamin Itoe

He was consecutively a Magistrate, a provincial Procurator General, Deputy Director in charge of Cameroon Bar Association, Director of Penitentiary Administration, Minister of Transport, Minister of Justice and Keeper of the Seals, Minister of Tourism, President of the Administrative Bench of the Supreme Court and also served as member of the special United Nations Tribunal for Sierra Leone. He is member of the Central Committee of the Cameroon Peoples' Democratic Movement (CPDM), the ruling party. The involvement of these people in politics encouraged more Bakundu to become politically conscious which enabled them to gain positions in government as District Officers, clerks and government contractors.

    The three men show that the Bakundu were acquiring a taste for politics and as power brokers were able to bargain for social amenities for themselves and Bakundu community like appointments to positions in government and employment of Bakundu children in companies and government ministries. If nothing else, the political careers of these men show the degree to which Bakundu are integrating into national politics and the national political culture.

Trade and Business
Prominent among successful Bakundu were men like Chief David Besingi, a Cocoa Buying Agent, and Chief David Motase Ngoh, a contractor. They competed with businessmen from other ethnic groups. They established businesses like provision stores, beer homes, restaurants, wholesale, retail and hardware stores. As far as the Cameroon economy goes, these are not minor achievements. Their success kindled the interest of other Bakundu to venture into business, including petty trade. We do not know how much money they made partly because they did not keep proper accounts and such confidential information for fear of incurring the envy, jealousy or accusations of witchcraft, not to mention tax liabilities. But judging from their improved standard of living they were successful, even rich, by the standards of their communities, and they were a testimony to effectiveness of the new ways of making wealth.

Since the first generation achieved literacy, became clerks, interpreters, messengers, pastors and businessmen, the pursuit of education in their families has continued in the succeeding generations. A good example is the Mediko family of Konye. John Mediko represents the first generation of educated Medikos. He completed elementary school at his village Konye in the 1920s. At the end of his elementary schooling, he developed a cocoa farm and was successful enough to use its proceeds to educate his children through primary school level. Meantime, he built a modern house and taught his son to read. He encouraged his friends who were reluctant to send their children to school, and eventually, many of them came to recognise the value of western education and did so.[199]

Frederick Itoe Mediko represents the second generation of the Mediko family. He attended Native Authority (N.A.) schools at Kurume and Kumba Town in the 1930s. At the end of his schooling, he worked for Cadbury and Fry, another agro-industrial complex as a clerk. He saved enough money, resigned from Cadbury and Fry, and became a farmer. He owned several cocoa farms averaging six acres each, became the first successful northern Bakundu businessman and a cocoa Licence Buying Agent, married four wives and had thirteen children. He eventually became chief of Konye, his village.[200]

Frederick Mediko

Frederick Mediko influenced his people in many ways. He lent money to people to pay for the schooling of their

---

[199] Conversation with Chief John Mediko III of Konye, Kumba, 20 July 2007.
[200] Ibid.

children. He refused to be a member of any secret society or association which he considered unprogressive. Rather, he spoke publicly of the value of adopting the Whiteman's ways. He built a modern home, and is considered the first northern Bakundu man to own a modern oven to dry cocoa. His appearance and modern dress was emulated by other Bakundu men,[201] like Etoto of Supe, who were encouraged by Mediko to work for the progress of their families through education. The village council provided him a platform for advocating his progressive ideas and criticising old ways he considered an obstacle to progress.

The third generation of Medikos consists of thirteen grandchildren whom he educated, because he was rich enough to pay for their education. Among the successful grandchildren is Mediko John Mediko III who succeeded him as Chief of Konye. When he completed his secondary education, he trained as an Evangelist and became a businessman. His brother is a Lieutenant Colonel in the Cameroon Armed Forces and the family counts two trained pharmacists, a medical doctor, an educationist and a state registered nurse.

The professional, business and career profiles of this generation are a measure of achievement and higher status based on merit not tradition. Taken together, they have also achieved further success by helping to educate members of the extended Mediko family. Like their parents and grandparents they have built modern homes, own cars, have generally improved their quality of life and the company they keep. Their impact on Bakundu society is best reflected in their ambition and drive and the emulation they have inspired in other Bakundu families.

The fourth generation of the Mediko family is made up of the children of the members of the third generation still

---

[201] Ibid.

studying in primary, secondary and high schools as well as universities at home and abroad. There is little doubt that the process, the achievements begun by the first generation have laid a foundation that is sustained and is likely to continue. The Medikos are only the most dramatic Bakundu success story.

Among other things economic success has permitted them to be mobile and travel in Cameroon and without. These achievements have given Bakundu purpose, ambition and creativity. They have become aware of the fact that anyone can make the most of the opportunities of life and enhance their status and well-being.

Forms of Marriage
The achievements of these families have consolidated a social revolution measured by successful blend of the old and new ways. This new way of life was reflected in their marriages which were essentially modernised traditional marriages which began with the traditional exchange of gifts and bridewealth that unite two extended families. Under colonial rule, innovations were introduced in Bakundu family and marriage life. Thus, marriages contracted during the colonial and postcolonial periods differed in setting and style from those contracted before.

We have already seen how the multiple experiences to which the Bakundu were exposed at home and abroad inevitably modified or changed some of their basic institutions. This was even more true of Bakundu marriage and family life. In contrast to traditional practices, modern Bakundu marriages were not "arranged" as in classical tradition with its prolonged negotiations between two kinship groups and not individuals. Once the man and the woman met and agreed to marry, they informed their parents. If the parents consented the date was fixed for the public ceremony.

Another aspect of these modern marriages that distinguished them from traditional Bakundu marriages was that they were monogamous and conducted in church. Payment of bridewealth was to be completed before the Christian ceremony took place. Sometimes, the marriages were civil ceremonies performed by a court Registrar, rather than in church or a home like the case of Andrew Ekuka Motanga and Margaret Sakwe, and Daniel Mukete and Josephine Lobe. Both church and court marriages involved conspicuous consumption and expensive ceremonies which were not characteristic of Bakundu traditional marriages. Increasingly, some of these marriages are trans-ethnic marriages. Such marriages include that between Benjamin Itoe and Mispa Ntuba and Nathaniel Bebe and Manga Bell's daughter. One significance of this type of marriage is that they bring people from different ethnic groups together and in this way creates strong sense of belonging between them. This, however, was not really a novelty since it had been going on for generations. Another significance can be seen in their offspring who cannot claim to belong to one culture – the father's or the mother's. The outcome is that in such situations a new cultural orientation begins to develop which eventually probably affects the traditional way of life of the couple.

The Westernised Bakundu children socialise mainly or as much as possible with the children of other educated Bakundu and non-Bakundu neighbours in the urban milieu. This evidenced the growing social distinction and class consciousness between educated and uneducated Bakundu. The modernised Bakundu are mainly civil servants and businessmen, petty traders, mechanics and drivers. In the towns where they are found they lived a relatively comfortable lifestyle which was reflected in their diet, dress and personal comportment, and the education of their children in the best state and private schools. Yet tradition dies hard and despite their new-found urban and semi-urban lifestyle, or perhaps because of it, they still offer libations to the ancestors and to honour the elderly. They did and do so in part because they knew how precarious urban life can be and felt the need to provide themselves with psychological security against its shocks. These shocks were received and cushioned by the Bakundu Improvement Union.

Bakundu Improvement Union

The Improvement Union's motto was "Unity, Sincerity and Progress". Membership was open to all Bakundu who paid their membership levy and any other dues. The main officers were the president, the vice-president, the general secretary and vice-secretary general, the treasurer and the auditor. Meetings of the union were held at least twice a year but executive meetings were held as often as the need arose.

The aim of the union was to lobby government for the improvement of their society; to award scholarships to deserving Bakundu youngsters; and to be generally concerned with anything that affected the welfare of the Bakundu. The union also assisted its members to find employment where possible, promoted the welfare and progress of the Bakundu and Cameroon as a whole.[202] Thus, the union was an index of the emergence of pan-Bakundu consciousness and solidarity.

The formation of Bakundu Improvement Union was an even more ambitious project along the same lines as the students' association and was also a direct result of the urban experience. Many Bakundu who worked in towns like Kumba, Tiko, Victoria (Limbe) and Buea, and those like Namata Ewanga, Rudolf Duala Itoe and Moses Ebollo who resided permanently in towns helped to form the Union. One of the underlying motives for its creation was to bridge the

---

[202] File No. Si 1953/2 5007. Bakundu Tribal Unions, Kumba Division. N.A.B.

gap between the Bakundu in towns and in villages. It was also intended to create a sense of oneness between the Northern and Southern clusters of Bakunduland. As noted earlier, its objectives were to promote the collective identity and interest of Bakundu, stimulate mutual assistance among new migrants and at the same time act like a training ground for future leaders.[203]

Joseph Esomba, a civil servant from Mabonji in Southern Bakundu was elected as its first president while E.A. Lenya, a teacher from Supe in Northern Bakundu was elected secretary. Annual meetings were organised in rotation in northern and southern Bakundu to provide an opportunity for Bakundu people to know their villages and understand their social problems. The last general meeting was held in January 1951 at Itoki in the north. Since 1951, after the Itoki gathering, no other meeting was held and in 1954 the Union collapsed partly due to ineffective leadership and the political climate then reigning in the Southern Cameroons.

In a manner similar to other ethnic groups, it raised funds from three main sources: member villages which paid ten pounds annually, individuals who paid one pound annually, and from donations, concerts, exhibitions and fines. The Union had branches in all villages except in new villages. There are no records of its total membership. But today, it has been transformed into Bakundu Cultural and Development Union in 2001.[204] The greatest achievement of the union was the solidarity and sense of belonging it promoted among the Bakundu.[205] The views expressed by some of its members testify to this.

---

[203] Ebune, *Political Parties*, 104.
[204] Interview with Namata Ewanga, Kumba, 10 July 2007.
[205] File No. Si. 1953/2 5007. Bakundu Tribal Unions, Kumba Division, NAB.

For example, John Nakomo of Mbu who worked with the Ministry of Health emphasised the union's role in raising Bakundu awareness to the usefulness of Western education.[206] Like Nakomo, Moses Ebollo emphasised the efforts of the Union to educate the people about the relation between education and development. In doing so, members directly and indirectly challenged unprogressive ideas and practices like witchcraft. He however regretted that the Union never encouraged thrift associations, like "Susu" or "njangi" to help members raise capital as was done by other ethnic formations.[207] Unfortunately, the union collapsed a few years after its formation because of divided loyalties.

The members of the Union were caught between supporting the Kamerun People's Party (KPP) of N.N. Mbile an *Orocko* man of the Batanga ethnic group and E. M. L. Endeley's Kamerun National Congress (KNC).[208] This divided their loyalties. The outcome was the extension of party differences to the Bakundu Improvement Union and the resulting tensions led to its collapse in 1954.[209] In terms of material achievement, it cannot with certainty be said that the Union achieved anything lasting, but it is remembered for its appeals to the sense of oneness and brotherhood among the Bakundu in an urban context where they found themselves as strangers.

In the immediate post-independence period, the Ahidjo regime urged Cameroonians to development through self-reliance. The response was the creation of the Bakundu Cultural and Development Meeting (BCDM) in the mid-1960s to strengthen the unity between the Northern and Southern Bakundu to join forces to lobby government for

---

[206] Interview with John Nakomo, Kwakwa, 8 July 2007.
[207] Conversation with Moses Ebollo, Kumba, 25 July 2007.
[208] Hansley Nagweya Ewane "The Bakundu Cultural and Development Meeting", B.A. Long Essay, University of Buea, 2005, 34.
[209] Ibid.

assistance to develop Bakunduland; to maintain and foster inter-ethnic and cultural ties, especially with *Orocko* in Ndian division.[210]

More recently, in its quest for the development of Bakunduland, this organisation was renamed the Bakundu Cultural and Development Union (BCDU). Since 2001 its focus has been to strengthen Bakundu solidarity, without which the goal of development of Bakunduland would be difficult to attain. In doing this, the association also aimed at competing with other such groups for the development of the Cameroon.

Many of these new social formations were a result of the Bakundu experience in towns and would not have emerged without that experience and the contacts with other people which it made possible. The nearest growing towns to which the Bakundu were exposed were Kumba, Tiko, Victoria (Limbe) and Buea. Kumba, with a population of over one million, was special because it was the chief town of Kumba Division and the closest urban community to any Bakundu village community. Kumba is particularly attractive and important because its autochthons, the Bafo, are also kinsmen with whom Bakundu share many cultural traits. This cultural affinity and geographical proximity no doubt made it easier for Bakundu to visit it or settle there more or less permanently, because it helped to cushion the culture shock that often accompanies relocation. The Bakundu went to Kumba town and other urban centres first to experience a new and freer style of life, to earn money to pay the bridewealth and meet tax-demands, and to socialise. These economic motives were bound up with motives of a personal kind as some Bakundu moved there partly to escape from a stifling village environment when it became intolerable.

---

[210] Constitution of the BCDM.

Kumba, like other towns, provided a variety of opportunities for self-advancement through civil service employment or in trading companies like the UAC. Others went there to be self-employed in petty trade or become carpenters, bricklayers, mechanics, drivers or simple casual labourers. In these towns, the desire to make money, acquire imported European luxuries, raise one's status in society or simply enjoy the bright lights were acquired values.

However one views it, the role played by urban or town dwellers to bring change to Bakunduland cannot be overemphasised. In some cases the experience of change is virtually daily. For example, the proximity of Kake to Kumba and the availability of modern transportation ease commuting and in addition to trekking the short distance, makes travel to Kumba relatively cheap financially. Visits to their villages by the town dwellers made their kinsmen to see the difference between village and town life. This changing pattern of migration especially among the semi-skilled, has been noted elsewhere in Africa, and is likewise motivated by economic and social factors. As Mirjam De Bruijn, Rijk Dijk and Dick Foeken note:

> The specificity of the conditions in areas that are marginal from both an ecological and economic point of view means that people develop economic and cultural strategies marked by a high degree of opportunism. The whole society is in fact organised around these opportunistic strategies.[211]

We have earlier discussed Bombe village in this study as a pioneer in westernisation through trade contacts with the Europeans, through education and missionary activity. In the long run, however, Kake not Bombe became the best

---

[211] De Bruijn, Van Dikj and Dick Foeken (Ed). *Mobile Africa: Changing Patterns of Movement in Africa and Beyond* (Leiden: Brill, 2001), 65.

example of the progress of westernisation and modernisation in Bakunduland. The main reason for this is its proximity to Kumba, the fourth largest and most urbanised community in Cameroon and certainly the largest urban community in the whole of the Southwest Region. Kake is two kilometres from Kumba and has a population of over eight thousand inhabitants.[212] The occupational base of the average person is farming, and administratively the village falls within the Kumba Urban Council. John Moki and John Sona both Bakundu from Kake, have been deputy mayors of the council. Most recently, following the 1997 reorganisation of the Kumba Urban Council now transformed into a City Council, David Makia Njumba, another Bakundu, is the second deputy mayor of Kumba III Council. This suggests the depth of Bakundu expansion and of integration into the rapidly expanding urban complex of Kumba.

Konye Village

The people of Kake are unique among Bakundu villagers; they consider themselves town dwellers. They enjoy facilities like pipe-borne water and electricity and have an integrated primary health centre while Kumba divisional

---

[212] Conversation with Chief Samuel Ndome, Kake Village, 27 July 2008.

hospital serves their more serious health needs. They commute to and from Kumba, shop in Kumba market which is the largest and the richest in the region; enjoy Kumba's facilities like restaurants and off-licence watering holes in the day and can return to the village by nightfall. The degree of urbanisation is particularly dramatized by the appropriation of the technology of music. Not surprisingly, through it the Bakundu have transformed their highly lyrical traditional rhythms into new genre of Bakundu pop music inspired, no doubt, by the example of the Duala and other similarly urbanised peoples.

Even more significant is the fact that some people live in Kake and work in town. Because of the ready availability of educational facilities like primary and secondary schools many Kake children do not travel out of the village for schooling. This helped to expose the children to modern education and reduced expenditure on schooling. On the other hand, this proximity of schools helped to reduce illiteracy. In fact, the creation of Teachers' Training Centre, Kake in the 1950s first provided a discernable impact on the Kake people as their children and those from other parts of the country came there to be trained as teachers. This produced an urge among the Kake people to embrace education for their social upliftment. It suggests that Kake is more nearly urban than rural, a fact which must arouse the envy of other Bakundu villages like Kombone Miso, Konye and Banga. Intensifying and expanding this trend is the fact that beyond Kumba, Limbe and Douala are more and more accessible, thanks to improved road transportation. Limbe can be reached in just over two hours and Douala in just over two and a half, while the less adventurous can reach Douala after a three-hour train ride from Kumba.

Such grassroots cooperation and solidarity helped to foster development in Bakundu villages with the encouragement of the union in 1970. At Ibemi villagers planned and completed two major projects by contributing over fifteen million francs to build a community hall and over forty million francs to build a bridge across one of the tributaries of the Mungo. The successful completion of these two projects strengthened the desire of the people to tackle other economic and social development projects. This ethic of self-development was emulated by other Bakundu villages like Mbu and Itoki. This was as a result of what the people had learnt under colonial rule to develop themselves by accepting new ideas and putting them into practice.[213]

Colonialism was thus a hands-on educational experience for everyone irrespective of social class. The experience of the Bakundu soldier paralleled that of the worker in the plantation. Both groups were expatriates: first and foremost, it enabled educated and uneducated Bakundu to learn new ways to earn a living even in non-traditional occupations like in cocoa, oil palm cultivation and trade which required the use of new ideas and technologies. Ultimately, the Bakundu learned new ways of raising and investing capital. Bakundu workers in plantations, for example, lived in an inter-ethnic environment. To adjust to the urban environment, they formed *njangi* groups in order to provide themselves some measure of financial security.

Bakundu Plantation Experience
Bakundu contacts with people from other ethnic groups particularly in petty trade were a learning experience. In the course of these contacts they learned new ideas and how to be more productive.

One of the first groups of Bakundu to be exposed to this kind of education was plantation workers with PAMOL, Elders and Fyffes, the CDC and Cadbury and Fry. This group included individuals like Thomas Bokuba, Daniel Dibo and

---

[213] Ibid.

Tobias Motuba. In these plantations, they were labourers, clerks, foremen, night watchmen or Field Assistants, all of whom were semi-literate. The plantations specialised in oil palms, rubber, bananas, tea, cocoa and pepper cultivation. Many took to petty trading and did some farming on land outside the plantations.

The most enduring result of Bakundu plantation experience was the education people received in the potential benefits of proper land management, cultivation of new crops, the use of chemicals and other technologies, and marketing of produce. The outcome was that when some of them eventually resigned or retired from the corporation they set up their own farms on which they applied this new knowledge. A good example is that of Frederick Mediko of Konye, who became a successful Bakundu farmer and agro-businessman.

This learning experience was not limited to the workers. It was extended to their children in schools provided by corporations like CDC where children were provided with formal education. This was another form of education or more precisely learning process under colonialism. It was a living experience for the Bakundu and other Cameroonians. Group interest was paramount in their dealings with each other. This was exemplified in 1947 with the formation of the C.D.C. Workers' Union by Dr. E. M. L. Endeley. The Union fought for better conditions of service for its workers.[214]

War Veterans

Apart from the experience gained from the plantations, those Bakundu who fought in the Second World War also impacted their people from what they learned abroad. A parallel

---

[214] For a full discussion of the CDC Workers' Union see Edwin Ardener, Shirley Ardener and W. A. Warmington, *Plantation and Village in the Cameroons. Published for the Nigerian Institute of Social and Economic Research* (London: Oxford University Press, 1962), 356-358.

experience occurred among Bakundu who fought in the Second World War like Ekole and Babunaka. Among Bakundu war veterans were Francis Elume Obie from Kombone, Benjamin Babiaka from Bole, James Njoku from Bole, Ebong from Bombe, Modika Akama from Dipenda, Eboa Ekole Modika from Mbu, and Benjamin Ngoe from Nake. Some had served in Burma, Israel, Egypt, France and Germany. They were recruited into the army partly because they were literate and semi-literate and when they returned home, they helped to educate their kinsmen to improve on their economic well-being. They were too few to form any association of ex-servicemen as elsewhere but as individuals, they influenced the behaviour of other villagers, especially by encouraging them to adopt European ways as the surest way of self-advancement.[215]

Generally, their experience abroad influenced their political outlook. They had seen first-hand the freedom enjoyed by Europeans and the economic progress that made possible a high standard of living for Europeans. Obie observed that although they achieved little that was tangible, the fact that independence was achieved opened a new era of opportunities for them.

Conclusion

European colonisers had one thing in mind – to create the framework for effective colonial rule. The presence of Europeans, businessmen, colonial administrators, the emergence of urban centres; construction of roads, the introduction of new laws, economic and social systems signified profound and inevitable change. Directly or indirectly, all of this impacted Bakundu culture and society. Whether consciously or unconsciously, Europeans began to

---

[215] Ibid.

transform Africa and Africans in their image presumably in order to improve the lot of the people.

Travel by Bakundu within and outside the country played a part in achieving this secular mission. The experiences were an essential to the pattern of transformation, in politics, economics and new patterns of community and personal behaviour. Inevitably, all these eventually affected all other aspects of Bakundu life. With people engaging in more diversified activities, their families and communities became transformed as more and more acquired more and better materials aspired to higher social status.

CHAPTER FIVE
FROM VILLAGERS TO TOWNSMEN

Introduction

Scholars have long recognised and written about the fact that between the two world wars and beyond, Africans, including the Bakundu, were increasingly exposed to and involved in a wide range of political, social and economic network and activities in urban centres. They also point to the accelerated pace of these developments as well as their ever-widening scale. This involved a double transition, physical and mental, that is difficult at best and risky at worst.

Urbanism

The term "urbanization" is used here in several different ways. It is associated with the process of population concentration in which the ratio of town dwellers to the total population in a territory increases.[216] Urbanization therefore takes place when a larger proportion of the inhabitants in a region come to live in the cities or towns. On the other hand, Peil defines urbanisation either as the proportion of the population living in non-rural places, the process by which these urban places grow, or the spread of a manner of life and values which have come to be associated with such places.[217]

According to Thomas Hodgkin, emerging towns acted as solvents, weakening traditional social ties and loosening the hold of traditional beliefs and values. The coastal towns provided opportunities for a greater degree of occupational specialisation, enabled men to acquire new skills and powers. By mixing people from a variety of social backgrounds, they made possible the discovery of new points of contacts and

---

[216] Kenneth Little, *Urbanisation as a Social Process* (London and Boston: Routledge & Kegan Paul Ltd, 1974), 4.
[217] Peil., *Consensus and Conflicts,* 254.

interest.[218] Moreover, the towns led to a degradation of African civilisation and ethics and contained the germs of a new more interesting and diversified civilisation with possibilities of greater individual liberty.[219] Increasing populations, new forms of socio-economic organisation, increasing control over the environment and improved technology are the principal factors responsible for urbanisation,[220] and all of these may have been applicable to African urbanisation. These are the factors that gave birth to the growth of towns in Southern Cameroons as elsewhere in the world. The impact of these factors was uneven, but it was evident everywhere including Bakunduland.

There are no big towns in Bakunduland so when we talk about urbanization we are talking about the fact that the Bakundu have access to big towns like Kumba, Limbe and Douala. It is along these roads that ideas and goods are carried along to villages. These ideas and goods which were consumed in Bakundu villages were a result of the creation of plantations that aided in the growth of the towns.

The development of privately owned and managed German plantations, and the emergence of the plantation economy in the Southern Cameroons before the wars introduced thousands of southern Cameroonians to a wide variety of economic activities and processes involved in this modern agro-industrial sector. Bakundu participated directly and indirectly in this sector as different categories of wage and salaried labour.

Being located in the South West Region of Cameroon and in divisions namely Victoria (Limbe) and Kumba, the plantations introduced those Bakundu who worked in them and lived in their vicinity to urban ways and the rhythms and

---

[218] Hodgkin, *African Nationalism*, 63.
[219] Ibid.
[220] Ibid.

processions of urban industrial production, however rudimentary their form. In other words, the plantations complemented the 'education' which Bakundu and other Cameroonians were receiving in schools with the experience of factory and field work. They inevitably learned about and transmitted the new methods of production-economy first practised in the plantations. At the end of the Second World War Britain transformed these privately-owned estates into a public corporation known as the Cameroon Development Corporation (C.D.C), the second largest employer in Cameroon before and long after independence,[221] alongside Cadbury and Fry and Pamol.

The labour force in the plantations did not come from the same region. People from other parts of the country and even from neighbouring Nigeria sought employment in them. Others came to do business. They were self-employed and lived close to the plantations. In this way the plantations were themselves part promoters of urbanisation as they helped to transform their vicinities into semi-urban communities with multi-ethnic populations. These masses of wage earners became an emerging proletariat. In the plantation vicinities of Victoria (Limbe) which were some of the most urbanised areas of Southern Cameroon, they were exposed to facilities like pipe-borne water, modern housing, healthcare centres and schools although not all of them enjoyed these amenities equally.

Furthermore, the plantations provided railways and roads which served the needs of the corporation and the populations around the towns of Kumba, the headquarters of Meme division. The people used these means of transport to travel freely to other areas but simultaneously the same transport facilities were channels through which information reached the people from distant places. The part played by

---

[221] For more on this, see Ngoh, *Cameroon*, 179-182.

the plantations in improving the Bakundu was also seen in the contributions made by the cooperative movement.

Cooperatives

Corporations were not the only modern Western institutions that brought changes in Bakunduland. The cooperatives also played a significant role in the development of Bakunduland. The first cooperative was created in the 1930s at Kake for cocoa farmers and was almost an instant success. Subsequently, cooperatives spread rapidly and by the 1940s grouped farmers together to market their produce, make it possible for them to benefit from government subsidies, as well as obtain loans to improve their farms and acquire inputs like fertilisers and insecticides.[222] The Konye Area Farmers Cooperative grouped all the Northern Bakundu villages. Southern Bakundu farmers were affiliated to the Kumba Cooperative Union of Farmers.

The creation of these cooperatives further transformed peasant agriculture among the Bakundu. According to Abraham Lokiri, Manager of Konye Cooperative, founded in late 1940 and still functioning up till this day, their introduction and government support was a great incentive to farmers.[223] It did good business for the farmers and over two hundred Bakundu registered as members. As already noted, they received subsidies for farm equipment, insecticides as well as loans which led to greater volume and better quality produce, especially cocoa. Although there are no statistics showing output of Bakundu farmers, there is little doubt that the amount of cocoa produced by the Bakundu was on the increase. Lokiri seems to attribute this to the fact that Bakundu now employed modern techniques in cocoa

---

[222] File No. Qd/a 1953. Southern Cameroons Marketing Board, Cameroon Province, NAB.
[223] Conversation with Abraham Lokiri, Kumba, 21 August 2006.

production and farmers like Zacharia Ituka of Wone now had larger farms averaging ten acres with a yield of over one and a half tons a year.[224]

Apart from the Kumba and Konye cooperatives, villages were also encouraged to form village cooperative societies in order to qualify them for assistance from government through the Southern Cameroons Marketing Board. The over twenty of these cooperatives did not do as well as anticipated for as Chief David Besingi noted, mutual suspicion and lack of trust in those who managed them led to their collapse.[225] Despite this collapse, the idea of cooperatives endured.

The Produce Marketing Board

An even more ambitious government initiative from which Bakundu benefited was the Produce Marketing Board created in 1953.[226] The main reason for its creation was to stabilise the incomes of farmers by fixing the annual prices of produce each year to anticipate and protect farmers against losses due to world market fluctuations. Its creation was also in response to persistent demands by Southern Cameroonians for regional status within the Federation of Nigeria. The Board did not make much tangible impact among the Bakundu initially. According to Adolf Nyangwe, who was produce inspector with the Board, many Bakundu, ignorant of better chances, sold their cocoa to agents who in most cases cheated them.[227]

The situation changed after independence when cooperatives dealt directly with the farmers. Bakundu villages again formed their own cooperatives and, to increase

---

[224] Ibid.
[225] Conversation with Chief David Besingi, Kumba, 24 April 2008.
[226] File No. Qd/a 1953. Southern Cameroons Marketing Board, Cameroon Province, NAB.
[227] Conversation with Adolf Nyangwe, Mile I, Kumba, 20 April 2008.

output of cash crops, the West Cameroon government encouraged cooperative officials to work in close collaboration with the Marketing Board which funded them.

One way the Board encouraged farmers was to pay them bonuses at the end of every cocoa season. The cooperatives sold the cocoa to the Marketing Board which had the monopoly of selling it on the world market. The amount of cocoa sold to the cooperative by the farmers was recorded after each sale.[228] A percentage of the profits earned was deducted and paid to farmers as bonuses usually after the end of the harvest season when the farmers tended to be in desperate financial straits.

Nyangwe noted that[229] when the Board began paying them, many farmers stopped selling their cocoa to middlemen and became members of the cooperatives. This new institutional arrangement raised and stabilised cocoa prices, improved the standards of living of the Bakundu and led to a corresponding rise in social status of the most hardworking among them. These bonuses ranged between twenty pounds sterling to one hundred pounds under British administration and twenty five thousand francs to two hundred and fifty thousand francs after independence.[230] They stimulated further investment in cocoa farming. Farmers like Bebe, Itoe and Mediko were the most notable of the Bakundu farmers whose success and prosperity based on cocoa farming encouraged others to emulate them.

A major result of these new economic incentives and opportunities was that it intensified competition among the Bakundu. Among the Bakundu, those who accumulated wealth competed for status within the society and were linked with possession of expensive luxuries like bicycles,

---

[228] Ibid.
[229] Ibid.
[230] Ibid.

gramophones, radios and ultimately cars by a few individuals and showed that acquisitive instinct was alive and growing stronger alongside the communal values of the Bakundu. It helped to create a new class of monied men like Chief David Ikoh Besingi. The "rich" Bakundu like Mediko, Itoe and Elangwe families have ensured that as many kinsmen as possible benefited from their status and wealth especially through the education of the children.

As he tells it, Daniel Dibo was a dramatic success story:

> We arrived Victoria after trekking for days from Ibemi. In those days there were no cars and even when these were introduced later, only the very rich could use them. We got employed in the German plantations as labourers. The place we went to for relaxation after a day's work was Victoria with its several attractions. In fact, if you did not visit Victoria town then you certainly were not in touch with modern times.
>
> My experience was enriching, especially as the plantations and the growing town provided a lot of opportunities for individual advancement. Using one's earnings wisely was the goal for many of us who left our villages, for if you failed those still at home would laugh at you as having been a failure. This fear made me work extremely hard and I am glad this success is seen in my achievements, a modern home and more importantly, the education of my children, who today, are independent and managing their own affairs. This is what leaving home meant

to many of us, an experience that was only gained by the hardworking individual.[231]

Such competition has driven the younger generation like Chief David Motase Ngoh of Supe, a contractor, and Henry Mukete, a young and forward-looking farmer from Kake, into new and more lucrative economic ventures like contracting in order to expand and consolidate their wealth and status. Some, less well known, have taken to petty trade and vocations like carpentry, bricklaying, sewing and driving. Competition has also taken the form of expanding farm holdings and building modern homes like Chief Martin Mokundu of Sambaliba. Inevitably, this new outlook entails the expansion of social needs notably the education of Bakundu children. Thus, economic competition has encouraged the recognition of individual achievement, the accumulation of wealth and the demonstration of individual merit, skills and abilities.

Land Speculation
There is however, a negative side to this acquisitive spirit and it has engendered the sale of land. One way the average Bakundu have tried to compete is to sell land as a way of getting rich quickly. Unfortunately, the wealth is often as quickly spent on conspicuous consumption. This tendency has been most common among the Southern Bakundu who are closer to the fastest growing urban centres where land values are higher because of the influx of people from other regions. This has sometimes contributed to frequent fraudulent land deals and expensive court cases. The sale of land has sometimes been due to the wrong belief that land is plentiful without taking into consideration human population and the variety of its uses, most especially farming and

---

[231] Conversation with Daniel Dibo, Tiko Town, 26 June 2008.

settlement. This wrong understanding has come to light in recent years, it is most obvious in Southern Bakundu villages with the constant influx of non-autochthons from other areas of the country and even beyond the national borders.

The paradox is that this is happening at a time when, as pointed out earlier, the Bakundu have become more aware of the value of land partly because of their plantation – urban experiences. Although statistics of Native court and traditional council proceedings dealing with land disputes are not readily available, their financial costs, not to mention the time they consume, is only the most obvious consequence of this trend. This is the price and evidence of how Bakundu are coping with the problems of complex urbanisation.

In Kombone Bakundu Customary Court, for example, several such land cases have been tried of which the following are typical.

FRO. C. R. BK. 1/79/80 PAGE 102
In the Kombone Bakundu Customary Court held on the 19th day of October, 1979 before:
1) S.M. Otte   President
2) D.N. Elangwe   Member
3) Chief E. I. Ebako   Member
1.100 francs fees paid in a C.R. No. 537627 of 11/9/79
Timothy Itoe plt. of 3/C Ekombe
Vis.
Chief H. N. Motia for Natives of Maromba 1
Statement: Title to land.
Particulars: Declaration of title to a farmland situated at Maromba 1 bush.
An order for defendant to quit from the encroached farm at once.
Claim: Not admitted
Both parties present.
Timothy Itoe, plaintiff, sworn on Bible states.

I am a native of Itoki Bakundu, now resident at Ekombe 3 Corners, and a farmer by occupation. In the year 1949 I met the villagers (natives) of Maromba 1 and acquired a piece of farming land. To this effect, they accepted and allocated a virgin forest to me. The elders of the village by then gave me the land to cultivate for my personal farm. I later on satisfied them according to native laws and customs of the Bakundu people by giving them a cow and wine. I then started cultivating the land and planting seasonal and economical crops. Upon all these years, I have been enjoying and making use of the farm without any problem for someone else, hence I have sued defendant to court to give me full title over the farm.

... COURT REMARKS

After recording evidence from both parties, plaintiff in his evidence acquired a virgin land from the Natives of Maromba 1 to cultivate his personal farm and this request was granted a virgin land was shown to him. As regards to native laws and customs of the Bakundu. Plaintiff did satisfy the villagers providing them a cow and wine etc. per-the evidence of the Chief of Maromba 1.

Following cross examination to Plt. Plt. has no objection to resatisfy the villagers accordingly following the customs. As regards to this, this court has no option on the title over the land, but confirms and awards title to Plt. over the land farmland in question.

... JUDGEMENT: For Plt for his farmland.

Plt to satisfy the villagers by providing them food according to Native laws and customs of the Bakundu people in practice.[232]

---

[232] FRO. C. R. BK. 1/79/80 PAGE 102. Kombone Customary Court Proceedings.

In a similar way Niyabe Emmanuel Eketi, Sakwe Martin Babiaka and Mejumba Victor as plaintiffs and Chief Ndome Mukwelle as defendant were involved into another land problem. According to Chief Ndome Eketi and Babiaka had encroached on his land claiming they had bought it. The matter was brought before the Kumba High Court which ruled as follows:

"REPUBLIC OF CAMEROON"
"IN THE NAME OF PEOPLE OF CAMEROON"
JUDGEMENT

The plaintiffs claim against the defendant "the sum of fifty million francs (50.000.000) FCFA being special and general damages for trespass to farmland, destruction and conversion". The background of the case is a protracted land dispute with a trial of claims, counterclaims and decisions. Although the case before the court is between individuals, the real issue is a dispute between natives and non-natives of Kake II. …I find that a case has not been made out against the defendant on the balance of probability. In the result, thus suit is dismissed. From all the circumstances of this case, I make no order as to costs.[233]

These are the only few of the many cases of illicit land sales involving Bakundu and non-Bakundu and among Bakundu themselves. As indicated earlier these cases have several implications like loss of valuable time and money.

The continuation of this trend, particularly among the younger generations, intensifies rural exodus and many

---

[233] Ref. No. HCK/41/95, High Court, Kumba – Meme Division, South West Province, Cameroon.

Bakundu will eventually become landless rural proletariat reduced to renting in a rapidly urbanising environment – a huge price of modernisation. The connection is simply that in villages like in towns they would experience the same urban pressures caused by unemployment and other urban phenomena. Already, for many youngsters, mainly school leavers, the movement to towns in search of employment and better livelihood is becoming a risky venture for those Bakundu school leavers lacking the appropriate skills to compete for the best jobs available. The end result has been frustration especially when they can no longer return to the village and to farming because they have sold their ancestral lands in the meantime. All this leads to alienation and anomie, all well documented phenomenon of urban-industrial civilisation. They therefore turn to casual jobs and temporary employment at best or to crime to survive. Mebu Mikeka of Mbu found himself in Tiko where, unable to cope with his problems died a disappointed man.[234] There are other tragic stories like his.

On the other hand, competition has also led to tension and conflict among the less successful Bakundu like school dropouts, University graduates and unsuccessful civil servants and businessmen like the Mathias Oponde.[235] The loss of his business contributed to his early death as he found it difficult to manage his home and pay back the debts he had. Nevertheless, a growing number of Bakundu in towns have forged ahead economically as evidenced by their involvement in economic activities which they once considered menial or unprofitable. George Mukete Ekambi, a painter,[236] admits he once ridiculed those who sat before a board to paint. His attitude changed when he saw one such

---

[234] Conversation with Thomas Ndima, Kake Village, 13 August 2007.
[235] Conversation with John Moki, Kake Village, 15 August 2007.
[236] Conversation with George Ekambi, Kumba, 15 August 2007.

painter whom he once denigrated selling his painting for what to him seemed like huge sum of money. It was then he understood that anything one did, provided it was well done, could fetch money. Today, he is a successful painter in Kumba.[237] In growing numbers, other young Bakundu are becoming mechanics, once considered a dirty profession, and Kemba Nakomo says he is proud to repair cars and gain knowledge of engines and someday hopes to own a garage. Manfred Etongwe, John Modika and Andrew Bekima are other examples of Bakundu, who like Kemba are technicians of all grades.[238] All these accounts show, Bakundu are competing successfully with other people for a secure place in the wider, complex urban world.

This changed and changing attitude of Bakundu towards economic activities they once considered undignified is clearly one result of their acceptance of and adjustment to urban / township life. An important side effect may well be that future generations will be less inclined to farming and other traditional occupations, especially as many youngsters who inherit farms which are generations-old family property are beginning to sell them mainly to non-indigenes.

Land and Labour
The implications of this development for the extended family are incalculable. Bakundu family and kinship relationships were/are examples of primal group solidarity that have been transformed in the pursuit of economic well-being and security. Such solidarity and cooperation is enhanced by the age-grade system which helps provide farm labour. This traditional form of labour mobilisation has gained more recognition since independence as an "informal" way of

---

[237] Ibid
[238] Interview with Vincent Esobo, Kumba, 16 August 2007.

using labour for economic purposes. This "informal" labour sector requires only enough money to provide entertainment and taken "wage payment" after completion of each specific task. It has the added advantage that the bond between members of the group went far beyond the immediate task and sometimes created and solidified inter-ethnic cooperation. As Paul Obase points out, "we too have now learnt what others do to help themselves rather than pay others who take our money away to develop their areas".[239]

Another result has been increased cooperation among the Bakundu. As joint activity in performance of specific tasks, cooperation implies recognition of mutual dependence and mutual benefit. Even the most individualistic Bakundu now recognise the need and value of such cooperation to achieve personal and common social goals. This is particularly true in the mutual aid associations known locally as *'njangi'*.[240] The prime importance of these associations is that they enable people without access to banks and other financial institutions to raise capital at affordable rates of interest. In urban centres where the Bakundu are found, Bakundu "Family Meetings" are organised on a similar basis for the same economic purpose as *njangi*.

Bakundu "Family Meeting" like the one in Buea, seeks to unite the Bakundu within the Buea sub-division in order to promote solidarity, to share mutual problems, to promote Bakundu culture and to ensure economic and the social well-being of members.[241] According to Jacob Maloba, President of the meeting, *Njangis* exist in the meeting. These *Njangis* are divided into several categories depending on the amount of money they are able to save monthly in these

---

[239] Conversation with Paul Obase, Ibemi, 28 March 2006.
[240] For more on njangis or savings associations, see P.C. Lloyd, *Africa in Social Change;* W.A. Warmington, "Savings and Indebtedness among Cameroons Plantation Workers", *Africa* vol. xxviii No. 4 1958, 329-343.
[241] Constitution of the Bakundu Family Meeting, Buea Branch.

round robin financial transactions. For example, there is one for monthly contribution of ten thousand francs made up of ten members and another for five thousand francs.

Whatever the number of members in each group the essence is that at the end of the year, each member receives his or her *njangi* savings plus interest earned on loans made to the members.[242] Such monies are invested in petty trade or used to pay schools fees and meet the cost of other personal and family expense, especially in emergencies. Catherine Mwengela, a housewife, pointed out how helpful her *njangi* group has been to her; the money she raised in this way helped especially to educate her children.[243] They gave assistance to the bereaved or sick or donated money to the kinsfolk of a deceased member. The money for this is/was raised from a special fund of the association styled as 'trouble bank', essentially an emergency fund to which every member made a yearly contribution.[244]

The *njangi* groups among the Bakundu in towns and villages have helped the Bakundu in several ways. Building on the traditional communal ethic these groups have reinforced group solidarity as the people have come to realise that they can work together for self-help, raise funds for individual needs, compete with other ethnic groups and thereby develop Bakunduland. The groups have raised awareness of the collective and more economic use of resources. As already noted, the desire by the Bakundu to develop themselves even with the limited means at their disposal has been, above, one of the fundamental change in attitude. Today, *njangi* groups have become a major way for the average individual to raise capital within and outside Bakunduland.

---

[242] Interview with Jacob Maloba, Buea, 25 September 2007.
[243] Interview with Catherine Mwengela, Buea, 26 August 2007.
[244] Constitution of the Bakundu Family Meeting – Buea Branch.

These initiatives have been complemented by government programmes. Thus, in an effort to expand agricultural production and curb rural-urban migration, the government instituted what has been styled Common Initiative Groups supervised and controlled by the Ministry of Agriculture. Farmers form groups averaging twenty or thirty members and apply for government assistance to grow crops like corn, yams, plantains, or raise livestock like pigs and rear poultry. Assistance from the government is given in the form of training and providing high yield seeds and agricultural tools and other simple, affordable technologies. One of such groups was/is the Kake Women Common Initiative Group.

These initiatives are indirectly related to urban and semi-urban life since they empower the Bakundu child in the rural and semi-rural area to profitably use his or her time and energy more productively rather than migrating to the towns where, because of lack of basic skills, he or she may not be employed. In this way, social ills like prostitution and petty-crime are avoided as many become conscious of the fact that even in the rural areas, with determination, success can be attained and opportunities broadened through hard work. With their proceeds in the rural areas they can still enjoy the benefits of urban living by visiting urban centres and acquiring what they need.

Alice Balemba, a social worker, confirms the economic benefits the Bakundu women derived from these schemes. According to her, Bakundu women and young men have learnt much about how to improve their livelihood.[245] Many like John Eboli, a young farmer at Ibemi, now know how to rear poultry, grow corn and mushrooms for commercial purposes, breed snails, all activities which keep them busy throughout the year. They have thus broken the

---

[245] Conversation with Alice Balemba, Kumba, 30 March 2008.

rhythms of traditional Bakundu lifeways irreversibly in their search of the modern, ideas learnt from those living in urban centres.

Predictably, in all these efforts they have created a new ethos of confidence that welcomes change in Bakunduland. The extent to which Bakundu have internalised the new modern attitudes and values discussed above is reflected in the younger educated generation and the new organisations they formed before and since independence in their effort to change Bakundu society for the better.

Under colonial rule these "schooled" elites formed various associations some of them short-lived. Some of these associations did not make any immediate tangible contribution to the development of the rural masses since their objectives were mainly to promote elite interests. However, some became advocates for expansion of education to rural areas especially in the immediate post-independence era. The ideology of the educational system did not change but the increased and increasing number of primary and post-primary schools as well as the increasing number of children who had access to them, meant that there were more literate Bakundu. It is this literate group who formed the Bakundu Students' Association (BSA) whose membership includes secondary, high school and university students.

The association has an executive body with a president, vice-president, secretary, publicity secretary, financial secretary, organising secretary; treasurer, auditors and advisers. Branches were established in villages in 1987 where the students had the duty to inculcate in their people the desire to send their children to school. The activities of these branches were reported to the central body which had authority to make and endorse all decisions affecting the progress of the association. The creation of branches in villages, Elomo Nakomo pointed out, was to ensure that students in villages behaved in a manner worthy of their education and of emulation by all Bakundu youngsters.[246] This was a model of top-down initiative for development.

Bakundu students were conscious of one thing: through education each individual and group was challenged to be as self-reliant as possible to show that the state and the people are partners in development and that each individual should cooperate. This heightened awareness, the result of education in the broad sense, contributed in 1990s to the awakening of Bakundu rural masses and expansion of their horizons by embracing education as the only tool for development.

To educate the people in these values, the association organises since the 1990s a "cultural week" once every year in a selected village. Among other things, their activities during the week included debates, clean-up campaigns, talks and lessons about health and sanitation and visits to neighbouring villages. All these grassroots activities reflect the students' commitment to change and contribute to the development of Bakunduland by awakening the masses.

A striking example of such awakening is represented by Maurice Ndo, a farmer. Inspired by what the students did at Koba, he could not hide his joy and he decided to send his children to school.[247] His decision led his friend, Motia, to regret that he had not educated his children even though he had the means.[248] There could be no stronger endorsement of education than this. However indirectly, therefore, the association was inculcating and spreading modern values. The new attitudes encouraged the learning of new skills and behaviour patterns, new myths of development, and the

---

[246] Conversation with Elomo Nakomo, Limbe, 26 March 2008.
[247] Conversation with Maurice Ndo, Wone, 26 August 2007.
[248] Conversation with Motia, Wone Village, 26 August 2007.

formation of groups like those cited above, committed to progressive change in Bakunduland.

Conclusion

The Bakundu urban experience was varied and had direct and indirect effects. The impact of urbanism on Bakundu individually and collectively was due to broader cultural forces. It has shown that these transformations were triggered by and took place in a rapidly urbanising context and was marked by continuity and discontinuity. But in the end, the net result of these multiple transformations was profound and irreversible because it was stimulated by a deep desire for a better life among the Bakundu.

Government institutions, private corporations and private businesses created an environment in which corporations like the C.D.C., PAMOL and Cadbury and Fry operated. The link provided a context that encouraged new ideas to thrive. The multi-ethnic environment provided by urban centres permitted exchange of ideas, borrowing and adjustments to a new lifestyle by the Bakundu who took advantage of the economic and social amenities urban centres and the CDC provided. All these encouraged and reinforced the desire and gave new meaning to solidarity. Taken together, these profound and multi dimensional changes, have remade the world of the Bakundu as they have done other African peoples beyond reversal.

GENERAL CONCLUSION

Essentially, this study is about culture change among the Bakundu from the time of their earliest indirect contacts with Europeans through Duala middlemen c. 1614, to the era of more direct contacts as colonized people under colonial rule and beyond to the immediate post-independence period in 1961. More precisely, it is about how the Bakundu struggled to preserve their ancestral ways, while responding to the social, economic and political demands and opportunities of modernity.

Ultimately, it is a story of continuity and change, of innovation, adaptation and adjustments whose end results, it has been argued, are the emergence of a new, semi-westernised Bakundu man, a new social ideal and a new culture that is neither purely or wholly traditional nor radically modern but a creative synthesis of the best of both worlds. To show the breadth and depth of this process, this work has examined the transformation of the socio-economic and religious institutions of the Bakundu and the adaptive capacity of their values under the impact of Western secular values.

This process of change among the Bakundu was neither uniform nor straightforward. There were gains and losses, and even contradictions for individuals and groups. Bakundu government and politics, economics and power relations under European rule initially benefited the chiefs and members of secret societies – the power elite. Like chiefs and elders elsewhere in Africa Bakundu chiefs, elders and secret societies who exercised power in traditional society lost their power to the colonial authorities. However, some of them gained new power, enhanced status and new territory with the support of the colonial regime under the N.A. system which earned them further prestige. Some used their new status to further monopolise and regulate the new trade and wealth made possible by European presence with or without the support of the secret societies.

Colonial administrations were not alone in impacting the Bakundu. Missionaries and the Missionary church played a large and significant role in this vast, profound and accelerating course of change. Religion was central in the life of the Bakundu. For this reason, the Bakundu initially fiercely resisted Missionary teaching and the effort to convert them. The resulting conflict was best reflected in missionary confrontations with secret societies and their hostility to traditional rituals and "superstitions". Sometimes it was the native converts, especially the catechists, who conducted these crusades against Bakundu religious practices and institutions. These crusades were therefore dramatic proof of the extent to which they had assimilated the new Christian ideas.

Although the new religion made converts who became catechists and pastors, eventually the vast majority of Bakundu Christians were of a younger generation who were educated in Missionary schools or worked in Missionary institutions like dispensaries. These people, many of them from the lower, underprivileged classes of Bakundu traditional society, formed a new social stratum. However, the depth of their commitment to the new religion varied and was sometimes doubtful. This explains why many of them still believed in witchcraft, performed traditional rites of passage and, when struck by crises, consulted diviners and traditional healers. Christianity among the Bakundu was thus essentially a hybrid religion, a synthesis of African and Western beliefs and practices. Nevertheless, it was another striking example of adaptation among the Bakundu.

There was another side of Christianity and the changes it introduced among the Bakundu. Christianity created multiple sources of tension between the traditional and the modernized elite, although the educated Bakundu continued to venerate the ancestors. They honoured the elders and chiefs but they also resented their power and control. In order to have the benefits of the traditional society, even some of them with university education and higher technical competence joined secret societies which were the traditional avenues to power, prestige and wealth. This may seem contradictory to the outsider but not to the Bakundu. It helped to resolve actual and potential social cleavages in Bakundu society, but also ensured continuity between tradition and modernity.

Education, defined as schooling and broader life experience, played a significant role in the direction and depth of transformation in Bakunduland as elsewhere in Africa. In missionary, government, N.A., C.D.C. and private institutions, and generally through various individual contacts with Westerners and Western ways, the Bakundu learned the skills of reading, writing and arithmetic. With these new skills, they were employed in growing numbers by missions, government, N.As and business firms as clerks, teachers, interpreters, catechists and messengers. In the long run, some became lawyers, politicians, administrators and businessmen.

What the Bakundu did not learn in schools they learned from cooperative organisation and other government-sponsored institutions like the Marketing Board which promoted cash crop farming, mainly cocoa, bananas and palm produce for export using modern technologies. These economic activities were encouraged and reinforced by commercial houses whose trade networks, however indirectly, sometimes reached the remotest Bakundu villages transforming many villagers into hawkers and petty traders. In this and other ways many Bakundu were integrated into a worldwide commercial culture that transformed them into modern producers and consumers and improved their standards of living. In this new culture and society, some of the more enterprising Bakundu individuals like Bebe of Banga, Itoe of Bombe and Mediko of Konye made enough wealth from these activities to become a new monied class whose lifestyle was distinctly elevated. They used their wealth to educate children of the nuclear and extended family and generally to project a new image of their people as ethnophilanthropists.

Having internalised the new secular attitudes and values of the wider world, they became the leading agents of change and modernism in Bakundu society. This process was reinforced, especially between the World Wars, by their experience as plantations labourers. Bakundu in small but growing numbers found employment in urban towns like Kumba, Limbe and ultimately Douala as mechanics, carpenters and petty traders. They lived in these towns permanently and semi-permanently, became as part of an urban proletariat. Although their economic lot might have been humble, they inevitably became models of new ambitions, striving and a new way of life created by successful adjustment and adaptation to these centres of Westernization. They were in different degrees urbanites.

Despite their successful adaptation, however, they did not abandon all their ancestral ways. Indeed, as individuals and groups they retained much in these ancestral ways and harnessed it to new purposes. They married in church or in civil ceremonies, across ethnic lines, but they paid bridewealth and performed required customary rituals. To help them withstand the stresses of urban living and to effectively compete with other ethnic groups they formed new associations based on traditional communal values of kinship solidarity and mutual help. Through the Bakundu Cultural and Development Association and its forerunners, they strengthened not only their solidarity but also their common identity in a multi-ethnic urban context. This consciousness of themselves would eventually enable them to participate in competitive national politics as a group through membership of political formations and parties. In independence and in post-independence politics a few like Chief Henry Namata Elangwe, Benjamin Itoe and Ebenezar Namata Ewanga became seasoned power brokers and politicians.

The emergence of basically elite associations like the Bakundu Cultural and Development Union and Bakundu Students' Association raised awareness of "Bakunduness" but it also involved the danger of creating an elite-mass cleavage in Bakundu society. To prevent this, the elites undertook to educate their less fortunate kinsmen and in the process helped to bridge the gap and to preserve and renew their cultural roots through innovations learned from elsewhere. Thus, the process of change begun by Westerners became irreversible but was now indigenized and directed by a Bakundu elite who belonged to both worlds, the traditional and modern.

Executive Meeting of BACDU

203

A Thatch House

Etana

Traditional Bag

Women's Dance

Male or Njoku dance

Ngoba Dance

Kata – A traditional stool for nobles

N. A. School Banga

Presbyterian Church, Kake II

BIBLIOGRAPHY

A – Primary Sources
1 – Archival Materials
National Archives Buea (N.A.B.)

Assessment Reports

F.B. Carr Assessment Report on the Bakossi Tribal Area, Kumba Division, Cameroon Province.

File No. Ae/37/807/22 Assessment Report on Bakundu and Mbonge Tribes, Kumba Division, Cameroon Province.

File No. Ae 37. Assessment Report on the Tribal Areas of Mbonge and Bakundu.

R.W.M. Dundas and F.B. Carr Assessment Report on the Bafo, Kumba Division, Cameroon Province.

R.W.M. Dundas and F.B. Carr Assessment Report, 1922 on the Bakundu and Mbonge Tribes, Kumba Division, Cameroon Province.

Intelligence Reports

File No Ae II Intelligence Supplementary Report on the Bakundu Area Kumba Division.

File No. 663/76/1923 A. Intelligence Report on the Bakundu Tribe of Kumba Division, Cameroon Province.

File No. Qd/a 1953/3 Intelligence Report on the Bakundu Tribe Kumba Division, Cameroon Province.

Reassessment Reports

A.A. Garson Esq. ADO Reassessment Report on the Tribal Area of Bakundu.

File No. AC61/143/1 vol. 1932. A.A. Garson "Reassessment Report on the Bakundu Tribal Area", Kumba Division.

File No. 143/1631 vol. 2. Reassessment Report of the Bakundu Clan in Kumba Division.

File No. 143/1 vol. Ae G1 Reassessment Report on the Bakundu Tribe Kumba Division.

File No. 143/1 vol. AR G1 A.D. Garson Esq. ADO Reassessment Report on the Tribal Area of Bakundu, 1931.

File No. 16265 Qh/C 1952 Southern Bakundu Native Administration Forest Reserve, Kumba Division, Cameroon Province.

File No. 13236 Qh/C 1936/3 Korup Administrative Forest Reserve, Kumba Division, Cameroons Province.

File No. Cd/192/1 Kumba Division Annual Report.

File No. Cd/1928/1 KDAR; 1927. Annual Report for Kumba Division.

File No. Qc/d 1917/1 Restriction as to palm wine and palm trees, Cameroon Province, 1917.

File No. 105/1921 vol. 1 Reorganisation of Native Administration, Kumba Division.

File No. 110/17/1932 Kumba Division of Separate Native Treasuries.

File No. 1524 Letter No. 1338/139 of February 20, 1935, Minutes of a meeting of Bakundu clan held at Ndoi in January 11, 1935.

File No. 3221 Ca 1948, Kumba Division Annual and League of Nations Report, 1950.

File No. Si 1953/2 5007. Bakundu Tribal Unions, Kumba Division.

PRO CR. BK 1/79/80 PAGE 102, Kombone Customary Court Proceedings.

Ref. No. HCK/41/95, High Court Kumba-Meme Division, South West Cameroon, Cameroon.

2 – Oral Interviews and Conversations

Balemba, Alice. Conversation with author, 30 March 2008, Kumba, South West Region. Civil Servant, Deputy Mayor, Konye, Aged 56.

Bebe, Victoria. Conversation with author, 16 August 2007, Kumba, South West Region. Retired Sonel Worker, Aged 68.

Chief Bebe, Emmanuel. Conversation with author, 2 November 2007, Banga, South West Region. Chief of Banga, Aged 63.

Chief Besingi, David Ikoh. Conversation with author, 16 April 2006, Kumba, South West Region. Chief of Ibemi, Aged 58.

Chief Mediko, John. Conversation with author, 20 July 2007, Kumba, South West Region. Chief of Konye, Businessman, Aged 56.

Chief Nakomo, John. Conversation with author, 26 April 2007, Kumba, South West Region. Retired health worker. Aged 78.

Chief Ndome, Samuel. Conversation with author, 27 July 2007, Kake II, South West Region. Retired school master. Aged 76.

Dibo, Daniel. Conversation with author, 30 November 2007, Tiko, South West Region. Retired C.D.C. worker. Aged 76.

Diongo, Andrew. Conversation with author, 15 March 2008, Douala, Littoral Region. Businessman. Aged 68.

Ebollo, Emmanuel. Conversation with author, 10 April 2008, Kumba, South West Region. Lawyer. Aged 42.

Ebollo, Moses. Conversation with author, 10 August 2006, Kumba, South West Region. Aged 72.

Ekambi, George. Conversation with author, 15 August 2007, Kumba, South West Region. Artist, Painter. Aged 56.

Ekoi, Peter. Conversation with author, 28 August 2007, Kumba, South West Region. Retired School Manager. Aged 65.

Ekole, Atinda. Conversation with author, 10 February 2007, Kake II, South West Region. Retired teacher. Aged 71.

Ekole, Johnson. Conversation with author, 27 July 2007, Ekombe, South West Region. Head Teacher. Aged 60.

Ekole, Ruth. Interview by author, 17 March 2006, Kumba, South West Region. Retired educationist. Aged 73.

Eseme, Akama. Conversation with author, 17 March 2006, Kumba, South West Region. Retired C.D.C. worker. Aged 75.

Ewanga, E. Namata. Conversation with author, 15 December 2007, Limbe, South West Region. Former Deputy of National Assembly. Aged 72.

Isoh, Abel. Conversation with author, 17 June 2007, Kumba, South West Region. Teacher. Aged 41.

Lokendo, Jacob. Conversation with author, 20 March 2008, Kake I, South West Region. farmer. Wone. Aged 78.

Lokiri, Abraham. Conversation with author, 27 July 2007, Kumba, South West Region. Retired Cooperative Inspector. Aged 66.

Maloba, Jacob. Interview by author, 25 September 2007, Buea, South West Region. Civil Servant on retirement. Aged 63.

Maloba, Joseph. Conversation with author, 15 August 2007, Buea, South West Region. civil Servant. Aged 55.

Molongwe, Elias. Conversation with author, 27 August 2006, Kumba, South West Region. retired health worker. Aged 70.

Moki, John. Conversation with author, 20 November 2007, Kake II, South West Region. retired Evangelist. Aged 77.

Motia, Abel. Conversation with author, 26 August 2007, Wone, South West Region. Farmer. Wone Bakundu. Aged 88.

Motuba, Joseph. Conversation with author, 18 March 2008, Buea, South West Region. Civil Servant. Aged 58.

Mwengela, Catherine. Conversation with author, 26 August 2007, Buea, South West Region. Housewife. Aged 60.

Nakomo, Elomo. Conversation with author, 26 March 2008, Limbe, South West Region. Civil Servant. Aged 40.

Namowango, Joan. Conversation with author, 15 August 2007, Buea, South West Region. Retired Civil Servant. Aged 60.

Ndima, Thomas. Conversation with author, 13 August 2007, Kake, South West Region. Ex-Serviceman. Aged 74.

Ndo, Maurice. Conversation with author, 26 August 2007, Wone, South West Region. Farmer, Ibemi. Aged 60.

Nganda, Rudolf. Conversation with author, 11 April 2008, Kumba, South West Region. Principal. G.H.S. Kake. Aged 48.

Nganda, Therese. Conversation with author, 20 December 2007, Buea, South West Region. Teacher. Aged 48.

Ngoe, Simon. Conversation with author, 19 December 2007, Kumba, South West Region. Farmer. Aged 56.

Nyangwe, Adolf. Conversation with author, 20 April 2008, Kumba, South West Region. Retired School Manager. Aged 68.

Obase, Ebenezer. Interview by author, 10 July 2007, Kumba, South West Region. Retired Teacher. Aged 61.

Obase, Paul. Conversation with author, 28 March 2006, Kumba, South West Region. Farmer, Ibemi. Aged 65.

Rev. Elangwe, Namaya. Interview by author, 3 May 2006, Buea, South West Region. Parish Priest, P.C.C. Limbe Parish. Aged 46.

Rev. Sakwe, Emmanuel. Conversation with author, 28 February 2008, Ibemi, South West Region. Retired Pastor. Aged 70.

1 – Books

Abraham, Aurthur, *Topics in Sierra Leone History*. Freetown: Leone Publishers, 1974.
Ajayi, J.F.A. *Christian Missions in Nigeria 1841-1891 The Making of a New Elite*. Evaston: Northwestern University Press, 1969.
Ajayi, J.F.A. and Michael Crowder, *History of West Africa vol. 2*. Ibadan: Longman Publishers, 1971.
Amaazee, V.B. *Traditional Rulers (Chiefs) in Cameroon History*. Yaounde: Press Universitaires, 2002.
Anene, Joseph C and Godfrey N. Brown, *Africa in the Nineteenth and Twentieth Centuries*. Ibadan: Ibadan University Press, 1970.
Ardener, Edwin. *Coastal Bantu of the Cameroon*. London: International African Institute, 1956.
Ardener, Edwin, Shirley Ardener, and W.A. Warmington. *Plantation and Village in the Cameroons*. Published for the Nigerian Institute of social and Economic Research. London: Oxford University Press, 1962.
Boahen, Adu. *African Perspectives on Colonialism*. Baltimore and London: The John Hopkins University Press, 1987.
Bohannan, Paul and Philip Curtin. *Africa and Africans*. Fourth Edition Illinois: Waveland Press, Inc., 1988.
Bruijn de, Van Dijk and Dick Foeken (Eds). *Mobile Africa: Changing Patterns of Movement in Africa and Beyond*. Leiden: Brill, 2001.
Buah, F.K. *West Africa Since A.D. 1000*. London: Macmillan Educational Limited, 1977.

Chabal, Patrick and Jean-Pascal Daloz, *African Works: Disorder As Political Instrument*. Oxford and Bloomington: Heinemann, 1999.

Chilver, E.M. and Ute Roschenthaler (eds). *Cameroon's Tycoon: Max Esser's Expedition and its Consequences*. New York, Oxford: Berghahn Books, 2001.

Collins, Robert O., James MacDonald Burns, and Erick Kristopher Ching (Eds). *Historical Problems of Imperial Africa*. Princeton: Markus Wiener Publishers, 2000.

Davidson, Basil. *The African Genius: An Introduction to African Culture History*. Boston: Little Brown and Company, 1969.

Ebune, Joseph B. *The Growth of Political Parties in Southern Cameroons, 1916-1960*, Yaounde: CEPER, 1992.

Gilbert, Erick and Jonathan T. Reynolds. *Africa in World History*. New York: Prentice Hall, 2004.

Goucher, Candice L., Charles A. LEGuin, and Linda A. Walton, *In The Balance, Themes in Global History*, Boston Massachusetts: McGraw Hill, 1998.

Gyekye, Kwame. *Tradition and Modernity: Philosophical Reflections on the African Experience*. New York: Oxford University Press, 1997.

Himilton, Carolyn. *Terrific Majesty: The Powers of the Shaka Zulu and the Limits of Historical Invention*. London: Harvard University Press. 1998.

Hodgkin, Thomas. *Nationalism in Colonial Africa*. New York: University Press. 1968.

Hopkins, A.G. *An Economic History of West Arica*, New York: Columbia University Press, 1973.

Ihims, Jacob A. *A Century of Western Education in Cameroon: A Study of its History and Administration (1944-1961)*. Bamenda: Unique Printers, 2003.

July, Robert W. *Pre-Colonial Africa: An Economic and Social History,* England: Davidson Publishing, 1976.

Keller, W.J. Schnellbach and R. Brutsch. *The History of the Presbyterian Church in West Cameroon.* Victoria: Presbook Printing Press, 1969.

Khapoya, Vincent B. *The African Experience: An Introduction*. New Jersey: Prentice Hall, 1994.

LeVine, Victor T. *The Cameroons from Mandate to Independence*, Berkeley and Los Angeles: University of California Press, 1964.

Little, Kenneth. *Urbanisation as a Social Process*, London and Boston: Routledge and Kegan Paul, Ltd. 1974.

Llyod, P.C. *Africa in Social Change*. England: Penguin Books, 1969.

Mair, Lucy. *New Nations.* Chicago: Chicago University Press, 1963.

Markovitz, Irving Leonard (ed). *African Politics and Society*. London: Macmillan Publishers, 1970.

Mbiti, John S. *African Religions and Philosophy*. Second Edition, New Hampshire: Heinemann Education Publishers, 1997.

Murdock, George Peter. *Africa Its Peoples and Their Culture History*, New York: McGraw Hill Books Company Inc, 1959.

Neba, Aaron Suh. *Modern Geography of the Republic of Cameroon.* 2nd Edition, New York: Neba Publishers, 1987.

Ngoh, Victor Julius. *History of Cameroon Since 1800*. Limbe: Presbook, 1996.

Nkwi, Paul N. *Traditional Government and Social Change: A Study of the Political Institutions Among the Kom of the Cameroon Grassfield*. Friburg: S.E. Friburgensia, 1976.

[Nyansako-ni-Nku]. *The Pioneers. A Century Picture Book 1886-1986*. n.d, n.p.

Odetola, T.O., O. Oloruntimehim and D.A. Aweda. *Man and Society in Africa: An Introduction to Sociology*. London: Longman, 1983.

Oliver, Roland. *The African Experience*. London: Pimlico, 1994.

Peil, Margaret. *Consensus and Conflicts in African Societies: An Introduction to Sociology*. England: Longman, 1982.

Plessis, J Du. *The Evangelisation of Pagan Africa. A History of Christian Missions to the Pagan Tribes of Central Africa*. Cape Town and Johannesburg: C. Juta and Company Ltd. 1929.

Redfield, Robert. *The Primitive World and Its Transformations*. Ithaca, New York. Cornell University Press, 1966.

Rodney, Walter. *A History of the Upper Guinea Coast, 1545-1800*. Oxford: Clarendon Press, 1970.

Rudin, Harry R. *Germans in the Cameroons, 1884-1914: A Case Study in Modern Imperialism*. New Haven: Yale University Press, 1938.

Rudin, Leslie and Brian Weinstein. *Introduction to African Politics*. New York: Praeger Publishers, 1977.

Spitzer, Leo. *The Creoles of Sierra Leone: The Response to Colonialism, 1870-1945*. Ile Ife: University of Ife Press, 1975.

Smythe, Hugh and Mabel M. Smythe, *The New Nigeria Elite*. Stanford, California: Stanford University Press, 1962.

Turabian, Kate L. *Manual for Writers of Term Papers, Theses and Dissertations*. 6th Edition. Rev. By John

Grossman and Alice Bennett. Chicago and London: The University of Chicago Press, 1996.

Vansina, Jan. *Paths in the Rainforests: Towards a History of Political Tradition in Equatorial Africa.* Madison: The University of Wisconsin Press, 1990.

2 – Articles

Chiabi, E. Mucho, "The Nigerian-Cameroonian Connection" in *Journal of African Studies.* Vol. 13. Number 2, Summer 1986.

Chilver "Nineteenth Century Trade in the Bamenda Grassfield" *Afrika und Ubersee,* Band XLV.

Comber, J.T. "Explorations from Mount Cameroons and Journey through Congo to Makuta" *Proceedings of the Royal Geographic Society* (New Monthly Series) vol. 1879.

Ebune, Joseph B. "Contributions of Self-Help Associations to the Growth and Development of British Southern Cameroons, 1922-1962: A Historical Perspective" *Epasa Moto. A Bilingual Journal of Arts and Humanities,* vol. 2 No. 1. Limbe: Design House, March 2004.

Warmington, W.A. "Savings and Indebtedness among Cameroons plantation workers", *Africa,* vol. xxviii No. 4 1958.

C – Theses and Dissertations

Atinda, Martin. "Bakundu Under Colonial Rule, 1897-1961". M.A. Thesis University of Yaounde 1. 2006.

Elango, Lovett Z. "Britain and Bimbia in the Nineteenth Century, 1883-1878: A Study in Anglo-Bimbian Trade and Diplomatic Relations" Ph.D. Dissertation, Boston University, 1975.

Eparh, Cyril Elad. "The Balkanisation of the Bakundu from Pre-Colonial to 1922: A Study in Underdevelopment M.A. Thesis, University of Yaounde I, 2005.

Ewane, Hansley Nagweya. "The Bakundu Cultural and Development Meeting", B.A. Long Essay, University of Buea, 2005.

Nyenti, Napoleon Ambi. "Bakundu Culture History: A Background Study". Post Graduate Diploma Dissertation in History, University of Yaounde, 1990.

D – Miscellaneous

Constitution of the Bakundu Family Meeting Buea.

Constitution of the Bakundu Students' Association.

Ebile, Marcus E. Letter of Appeal to Supervisor of Basel Mission Schools, Southern Cameroons.

Mosongo, A.K. "Keynote Address presented by the Congress Bureau of the Bakundu Cultural and Development Meeting on the occasion of their 14th Annual Gathering at Bole-Dipenda on the 18th of January 1987.

Smith, Edwin W. The Christian Mission in Africa: A Study Based on the Work of the International Conference at Le Zoute, Belgium, September 14th to 21st, 1926.

www.ingramcontent.com/pod-product-compliance
Lightning Source LLC
Chambersburg PA
CBHW072235290426
44111CB00012B/2100